Jim Blankenship, CFP®, EA

NO LON
PROPER
PROPER

A
Social Security
Owner's Manual

YOUR GUIDE TO
SOCIAL SECURITY
RETIREMENT, DEPENDENT'S
AND SURVIVOR'S BENEFITS

Copyright © 2011, 2013, 2014 by Jim Blankenship, CFP®, EA

A Social Security Owner's Manual

By Jim Blankenship, CFP®, EA

ISBN 978-1505396607 / 1505396603

All rights reserved solely by the author. The author guarantees all contents are original and do not infringe upon the legal rights of any other person or work. No part of this book may be reproduced in any form without the permission of the author. The views expressed in this book are solely the views of the author and do not represent the views of the publisher.

Reproduction or translation of any part of this work beyond that permitted in Section 107 or 108 of the 1976 United States Copyright Act without the permission of the copyright owner is unlawful.

Use of the words "Social Security", "Social Security Account", "Social Security System" or "Social Security Administration" in this work should not be in any way interpreted or construed as approval, endorsement or authorization by the Social Security Administration, the Centers for Medicare and Medicaid Services, or the Department of Health and Human Services, or that the author has some connection with or authorization from the Social Security Administration, the Centers for Medicare and Medicaid Services, or the Department of Health and Human Services. It must be understood that all specific facts and rules explained in this book are freely available from the Social Security Administration.

Every effort has been made to ensure this publication is as accurate and complete as possible. However, no representations or warranties are made with respect to the accuracy or completeness of the contents of this book. It is not the intent of this publication or its author to provide professional tax, investment or legal advice. The strategies contained herein may not be suitable for your situation. You should consult with a professional where appropriate. This publication should only be used as a general guideline and not as the ultimate source of information regarding Social Security.

Requests for permission or further information should be directed to the author via email at Jim@BlankenshipFinancial.com.

About the author

Jim Blankenship is a financial planner based in New Berlin, Illinois. Through his Fee-Only financial planning practice, Jim provides unbiased financial advice to individuals from all walks of life.

Jim Blankenship, CFP®, EA

Jim@BlankenshipFinancial.com

Praise for
A Social Security Owner's Manual

The "everyman's guide" to Social Security. A must-read for anyone who wants to maximize their available benefits.
    – Kathleen Campbell, CFP®, *Campbell Financial Partners, LLC*

A clear explanation of the many options that every participant should consider before making an application for benefits.
    – Wayne Koppa, *Scout Financial Planning*

A "must have" reference book for financial advisors and a "must read" book for anyone who wants to get the most out of their Social Security benefits.
    – Allison Stutts, CPA, *A.M. Stutts Financial Management, LLC*

The most straightforward guide I've found for determining the best Social Security strategies for married couples. Jim's examples really clarify this tricky issue - thanks Jim!
    – Kathy Hankard, CFP®, *Fiscal Fitness, LLC*

Jim Blankenship has written a definitive guide to understanding and managing arguably the largest and most important component of the American retirement income. Making decisions about social security without consulting this book could cost hundreds of thousands of dollars over your lifetime or the lifetime of your clients.
    – Jason Lampert, Candidate for CFP®, *Lucid Life Planning*

Dedication

This book is dedicated to my wife Nancy, who never fails to amaze me with her resilience, courage, and boundless love.

Acknowledgements

It is no small matter to acknowledge the efforts one's colleagues. This group astounds me with the selfless ways that they pitch in. I know firsthand the level of activity that this group faces on a day-to-day basis from conversations with many of them, but they never hesitated to invest their time and talents into the review, editing, and fact-checking of this book.

Listed below are the folks who specifically lent a hand on this edition, so I thought I'd mention them by name:

Andy Tilp, Michael Timmerman, Tom Nowak, Buz Livingston, Steve Ellisor, Shawn Koch, David Barnett, Lea Ann Knight, Kathleen Campbell, Josh Giminez, Mike Piper, and Sterling Raskie.

There are many others to acknowledge that I couldn't start to list because I'm certain I'd overlook some, but if you've had a hand in this book, the thanks goes to you as well.

You will never know just how much you all mean to me – you have helped to produce a coherent guide from my ramblings; you've reined in my silly sense of humor when needed; you've made this book far better than it should have been. Most of all you've been good friends and brilliant colleagues, encouraging and inspiring me all along the way. Thanks for everything!

Table of contents

Foreword xv
Introduction xix
Part 0: Primer 1
The Ground Rules 1
Part 1: The Basics 5
The Basic Components..5
1. Eligibility..5
2. Full Retirement Age 9
3. Average Indexed Monthly Earnings (AIME)....................11
4. Primary Insurance Amount (PIA) 15
5. Bend Points 19
Calculations..23
6. Calculating Your Retirement Benefit................................23
7. Calculating the Spousal Benefit 27
8. Calculating the Survivor Benefit.....................................31
9. Calculating the Family Maximum Benefit........................39
10. The Impact of Zero Years 43
11. Making Every Month Count 45
Disability Benefits...47
12. Eligibility for Disability Benefits..................................47
13. When You've Stopped Working.....................................51
14. Disability Benefits at Retirement 53
15. Family Maximum Benefit for Disability.........................55
Part 2: Reductions 57
Earnings Reductions 57
16. Earnings Tests 57
17. The year you begin benefits 59
18. Earnings Test is Specific to the Individual....................61
19. Payback When You've Earned Too Much......................63
GPO and WEP..65
20. Windfall Elimination Provision.....................................65
21. Government Pension Offset 69
22. When GPO and WEP Apply 73
Taxes...75
23. How Social Security Benefits Are Taxed........................75
Part 3: The Administration 79
24. Talking to the Social Security Administration 79
25. Checking Your Social Security Benefit 81
26. Your Social Security Benefit Statement.........................83

27. How COLAs Are Calculated..87
28. Withholding for Your Social Security............................91
Part 4: Tips and Strategies 95
29. Retiring Early 95
30. Should I Use IRA Assets or Social Security Benefits?............99
31. The Do-Over..103
32. History of the Do-Over..105
33. Spousal Benefits in Cases of Divorce 107
34. Remarriage and Spousal Benefits................................111
35. Delayed Benefits 113
36. A Twist on Spousal Benefits.......................................117
37. File and Suspend 121
38. Deemed Filing 125
39. Coordinating Spousal Benefits...................................129
40. Spousal Coordination Scenarios................................131
41. More Spousal Coordination Scenarios 139
Part 5: The Future of Social Security 145
42. Solvency..145
43. Methods of Calculation of COLAs 151
Acronyms..155
Appendix A..157

Table of tables

Full Retirement Age 10
Average Indexed Monthly Earnings... 12
Bend Points 21
Maximum and Minimum Factors Based on Age 25
Reduction Factors for Spousal Benefits 29
Family Maximum Benefit Bend Points....................................... 41
Recent Work and Duration of Work Credits.............................. 48
Taking Social Security Benefit at Age 62 100
Taking Social Security Benefit at Age 66 100
Taking Social Security Benefit at Age 70 101
Maximum and Minimum Credit Adjustments 114
Spousal Coordination Survivor Benefit Example 131

Foreword

Type the word "retirement" into your favorite web browser and you'll easily tap into over 200,000 webpages. And two of the top, non-advertised sites, are for the Social Security Administration. That seems appropriate considering the importance of Social Security to the success of our retirement plans. You can get all of the information you should ever need to know about retirement in just 0.02 seconds. Or maybe not…

We live in an age of nearly instant access to information. This information may be from great articles or mind expanding academic research, or simply the opinions of anonymous individuals who feel entitled to respond authoritatively to others' research and publications.

More information doesn't necessarily translate into better financial decision making. The overload is actually counterproductive. Whether the subject is determining if you can afford to retire, or how best to fund your retirement income needs, you'll find the complete spectrum of opinions on the web. I didn't say digesting this information and turning it into usable knowledge for your situation was going to be easy. It's just readily available.

On the web or in a printed publication, it's not necessarily inappropriate to have different viewpoints on a subject involving personal finance. However, personal financial planning is something altogether different. It's very personal and it's all about planning. The finance part is the only overlapping component. Of course there are concrete rules that apply to certain subjects, like taxes and eligibility requirements. But, the most important issues have to do with your personal circumstances, and how you and your family would best be served under various strategies or approaches. This is the essence of personal financial planning... knowing how to apply information in the most appropriate ways to accomplish what matters most in your life.

Okay, so I've made the argument for not wasting time surfing the Internet if you want specific advice or answers tailored to your personal circumstances. But, how do you know what questions to ask or even where to start? Who can you trust to know and do what's best for you? These are all very important questions. The more knowledge you have of your financial situation and the options available to you, the more successful you will be. This is true even if you're a do-it-yourselfer or if you're working with a professional financial planner.

Information is not knowledge. Wisdom is knowledge and knowledge is power! A professional financial advisor serves a very important role in our society and possibly in your life. But, they shouldn't have all the power. Remember - no one will look after your money better than you will.

Arm yourself with the knowledge to ask the important questions, be able to make informed decisions and to select the most appropriate advisor for you... if and when you need one. This little book is a great start. It's concise, easy to read, and packed with the knowledge you need to best take advantage of the Social Security system. A Social Security Owner's Manual is the most refreshing, enjoyable, and directly applicable resource I've ever read on the subject. Invest the time to gain this essential knowledge. You and your retirement lifestyle will be glad you did!

Sheryl Garrett, CFP®, AIF®

Founder of the Garrett Planning Network

Award winning author/co-author of:

Garrett's Guide to Financial Planning (National Underwriter 2002, 2007)
Just Give Me the Answers (Dearborn Trade 2004)
Money without Matrimony (Dearborn Trade 2006)
Personal Finance Workbook For Dummies® (Wiley 2007, 2012)
A Family's Guide to the Military For Dummies® (Wiley 2008)
Investing in an Uncertain Economy For Dummies® (Wiley 2008)

Introduction

It must be understood at the outset that as the author of this book I have no connection with or authorization from the Social Security Administration, the Centers for Medicare and Medicaid Services, or the Department of Health and Human Services. Use of the words "Social Security", "Social Security Account", "Social Security System" or "Social Security Administration" in this work should not be in any way interpreted or construed as approval, endorsement or authorization by the Social Security Administration, the Centers for Medicare and Medicaid Services, or the Department of Health and Human Services.

The facts in this publication are freely available from the Social Security Administration. The organization, interpretation, and explanation of these facts have been developed over years of study by the author of the facts and rules of the system. It is the organization, interpretation and explanations that provide the value in this work.

Social Security has become a significant part of many retirees' sustenance, ever since it was first introduced back in the 1930's. As the traditional pension plan goes the way of the buggy-whip and common investor behavior leads to poor results in savings plans (if there are any savings at all!), the Social Security benefit becomes more and more important.

Unfortunately, the way Social Security works is a mystery for most folks. There's really not much in the way of guidance for using the system. Relying solely on the phone representatives from the Social Security Administration for guidance is bound to lead you to a less-than-optimal result. The problem is that the SSA staff are not trained to optimize or help you to plan your benefits, they are trained to help you apply for benefits *right now.*

As with most financial activities, it pays to learn as much as you can about your options, possible strategies, and the pluses and minuses of various choices you can make. This book provides you with the groundwork to better understand the Social Security system so you can at least be well-informed about your options as you approach the date when you begin taking benefits.

I hope this book is useful as well as entertaining. I've done my best to ensure that the information contained herein is accurate and correct as of presstime – but laws change quickly and limits are adjusted annually. Look for updates to this material at

www.SocialSecurityOwnersManual.com

In addition to the annual adjustments to figures, I've received a great deal of feedback from readers of the previous editions of the book. There have been many recommendations for additional examples, more clarification, and other situations to be considered. I have taken each and every piece of feedback into consideration as I've produced this edition, and so I hope the improvements are helpful.

How to use this book

This book deals primarily with Social Security retirement and survivor's benefits. Disability benefits are only briefly discussed.

In addition, while I've gone to great lengths to provide a comprehensive guide to the Social Security retirement benefits system, I've also been accused of providing instructions for building a clock when many folks only want to know what time it is.

Considering the diverse interests of those who may be reading this book, below is a guide to the parts of the book to help you navigate.

Part 0: Primer is a list of some building-block rules that are important to understand. Buzz through this list quickly (it's short) on the start, but plan to refer back to it as you learn more.

Part 1: The Basics is all about the inner workings of calculations used to determine benefit amounts. This section is good for financial advisors, attorneys, accountants, and others who would like a better understanding and a reference for how it all works.

Part 2: Reductions explains the various reductions that can impact your Social Security benefits. Included here are the Earnings Test, GPO and WEP, and how taxation of Social Security benefits works.

Part 3: The Administration details information about working with the Social Security Administration. For example, if you are having difficulty with your benefit application, this section may help you.

Part 4: Tips and Strategies is where you'll find tips and strategies that you might use in developing your Social Security benefit plans. This section may be the most useful for the average reader, while the other sections provide supporting information.

Part 5: The Future of Social Security is where I dust off the crystal ball and provide you with some guesses as to what may be coming for the future of Social Security. This part is probably the least useful as it's bound to be inaccurate five minutes after the book is printed, but it makes for a nice round number of "Parts".

Part 0: Primer

The Ground Rules

There are certain rules that will be helpful to fully accept as facts while you learn about your Social Security benefit. If this is your first reading of the book, skim down through this list before moving on. Don't expect to fully understand these rules on the start – but keep in mind you might want to refer back to this list of Ground Rules from time to time so that you can keep things straight.

Basic Social Security Rules

- The earliest age you can receive retirement benefits is 62.

- The earliest age you can receive Survivor Benefits is 60 (50 if you are disabled).

- Filing for any benefit before Full Retirement Age will result in a reduction.

- Your spouse must have filed for his or her retirement benefit in order to enable you to file for Spousal Benefits.

- File & Suspend and filing a Restricted Application are two distinctly different things.

- The earliest age that you can File & Suspend is your Full Retirement Age.

- The earliest age that you can file a Restricted Application is your Full Retirement Age.

- You cannot File & Suspend and file a Restricted Application at the same time.

- While technically allowed, there is very little accomplished if both spouses File & Suspend. Typically one spouse will File & Suspend and the other will file for Spousal Benefits based upon the first spouse's record.

- On the other hand, only one member of a married couple can file a Restricted Application. The exception to this rule is for divorced spouses who remain unmarried – and are both over Full Retirement Age.

- If you have filed for your own benefit prior to Full Retirement Age and are therefore receiving a reduced benefit by filing early, when you file for a Spousal Benefit you will never receive the full 50% of your spouse's Primary Insurance Amount.

- For every month after Full Retirement Age that you delay filing for your own retirement benefit, you will accrue Delayed Retirement Credits, increasing your future retirement benefit when you file for it.

- There is no increase to Spousal Benefits if you delay filing beyond your Full Retirement Age.

- There also is no increase to Survivor Benefits if you delay filing beyond your Full Retirement Age.

Part 1: The Basics

The Basic Components

The basics. This is the logical place to begin your journey of learning more about your Social Security benefits. As with building a house, a solid foundation is important to support the finished product. Don't feel like you need to understand every nuance of these basic components at the start. Use this portion of the book as a reference – review in the beginning, and then refer back to help you understand some of the later sections which apply these basics.

1. Eligibility

It's important at the outset to understand how you can become eligible for Social Security benefits so you are clear about the requirements.

In order to be eligible to receive Social Security benefits – whether retirement, disability, or survivor – a worker must earn the eligibility to receive benefits. The general rule of thumb for the worker born in 1929 or later is: to receive full benefits he or she must earn at least 40 quarters of credit within the system. (If you were born before 1929 and you're reading this book you really should find a hobby!)

Social Security Credit

A quarter of Social Security credit is earned for each $1,220 earned per calendar quarter (in 2015). This amount is indexed each year – for example, the amount of earnings for a credit in 2014 was $1,200. So if a worker earns at least $4,880 in 2015 (doesn't have to be spread over the four quarters), four quarters of credit are earned with the Social Security system. The maximum number of credits earned in any year is four.

Minimum Credits

The minimum number of quarters of credits for retirement benefits, as mentioned above, is 40 for anyone born in 1929 or later.

For disability benefits if you become disabled before age 62 these benefits may be available to you if you have at least six quarters of credits earned. Your disability benefits may be reduced from the maximum based upon your age and how many credits you happen to have earned.

For example, if you've only earned the minimum 6 credits and you're under age 24 when you apply for disability benefits, you are eligible for full disability benefits. As your age increases the minimum credits for full disability benefits increases to the maximum requirement of 40 credits by age 62 – ten years' worth.

See Chapter 13 for a more complete explanation of how this works.

Eligibility for Spousal Retirement Benefits

If you are married to someone who has filed for benefits, you've been married to this person for at least 12 months, and you are at least age 62 – you are qualified to receive Spousal Benefits.

Additionally, if you are divorced (and not remarried) and you were married to the eligible worker for at least ten years, you can be eligible for Spousal Benefits based upon your former spouse's record - as long as you remain unmarried. Your ex-spouse must be eligible for benefits, meaning he or she must have the required quarters of coverage and is at least age 62. Your ex doesn't have to be actively receiving benefits – but if the ex has not filed for benefits, you must have been divorced for at least two years to be eligible. Lastly, you must be at least age 62. The same rules apply as if you were still married, except your ex-spouse doesn't have to apply for benefits in order for you as a divorced spouse to be eligible for the Spousal Benefit. If the ex-spouse has already filed for benefits, the two-year rule (after the divorce) does not apply.

However - if you remarry at any time while your ex-spouse is still alive you will become ineligible for the Spousal Benefit while you remain married. If there is a subsequent divorce or the current spouse dies, your eligibility is restored – and you can apply for Spousal Benefits on either ex-spouse's record as long as you meet the criteria. If the first spouse (or any earlier spouse) dies, the widow(er) becomes eligible for a Survivor's Benefit as a Widow(er) (however, see remarriage rules for widow(er)s in Chapter 34). You can choose any earlier spouse (if you were married more than once) for your Spousal and/or Survivor Benefit - as long as you meet the length of marriage eligibility test with that former spouse. You can also switch to a different ex-spouse later if the other ex-spouse meets the requirements and switching would result in a larger benefit.

Note that I said "you can choose <u>any</u> earlier spouse" above in reference to the situation where you may have been married more than once for the minimum 10 years. You are limited to *only one former spouse's benefits at a time*. You could not collect two or more ex-spouses' benefits at once.

Eligibility for Children

If the worker is currently enrolled for benefits (again, the worker could have suspended[1] receiving benefits), a child under age 18 who is a dependent of the worker would be eligible to receive benefits based upon the worker's   record.

---

[1] Suspending benefits is a tactic allowed at Full Retirement Age which provides a worker the option to establish a record with the SSA. This record allows dependent's and spouse benefits to be claimed on the worker's record, while allowing the worker to earn Delayed Retirement Credits. See Chapter 37 for more details.

2. Full Retirement Age

The Full Retirement Age or FRA (gotta love the government for their acronyms!) is a key figure for the individual who is planning to receive Social Security retirement benefits. Back in the olden days when Social Security was first conceived FRA was always age 65.

Then in 1983 the Social Security Act was amended to make changes to the FRA. Beginning with folks born in 1938 the FRA would be increased as shown in the table on the next page. For folks born in 1960 and beyond, FRA is age 67 (as of this writing) but don't expect this figure to remain the top forever. Increasing the FRA is one way to reduce the cost of the overall program, which is a constant concern for the government since this program presently amounts to more than half a trillion dollars in payout every year.

What's interesting is, even though the FRA has been increasing, the "early" retirement and "late" retirement ages have remained the same, at 62 and 70, respectively. I suspect at some stage those ages may be adjusted as well, recognizing that life expectancy has trended upward, as well as to improve the fiscal outlook of the program in general.

The following table displays the current FRA ages by year of birth:

Full Retirement Age

Year of Birth	FRA
1943-1954	66
1955	66 and 2 months
1956	66 and 4 months
1957	66 and 6 months
1958	66 and 8 months
1959	66 and 10 months
1960 or later	67

Source: Social Security Administration

Note: persons born on January 1 of any year should refer to the FRA for the previous year.

3. Average Indexed Monthly Earnings (AIME)

Another key component in determining your Social Security retirement benefit is called the Average Indexed Monthly Earnings or AIME (there's another acronym - get used to it). The AIME is calculated by taking the 35 years of your working life with the highest earnings (adjusted for inflation) while paying into Social Security and then computing an average of those indexed amounts. This is done by adding up all of the indexed earnings amounts and dividing by 420.

Gobbledy-gook, right? Okay, here's another way to explain it: as you work in a Social Security-covered job your earnings are recorded each year. Each year the SSA applies an inflation factor to the earnings for the year, based upon the Average Wage Index (AWI, more on this later). These indices for each year of your earnings are adjusted annually, reflecting the new AWI applied.

Once you are eligible for retirement (age 62, your Earliest Eligibility Age, or EEA), these years of earnings are put into a table and the indexes applied. On page 12 is an example of an earnings table with indices applied. Keep in mind that this table will look different for each year of birth. The table is based on an individual who reached age 62 in 2008, born in 1946.

Average Indexed Monthly Earnings

Age	Earnings	Index	Indexed Earnings
22	$ 5,000.00	7.4186559	$37,093.28
23	$ 5,589.41	7.0133446	$39,200.47
24	$ 5,771.91	6.6817598	$38,566.51
25	$ 5,951.90	6.362084	$37,866.51
26	$ 6,259.69	5.794243	$36,270.16
27	$ 6,598.18	5.453047	$35,980.19
28	$ 6,724.29	5.147081	$34,610.48
29	$ 7,263.44	4.789173	$34,785.89
30	$ 7,652.52	4.480037	$34,283.57
31	$ 8,151.79	4.226722	$34,455.35
32	$ 8,771.10	3.915769	$34,345.61
33	$ 9,095.79	3.600777	$32,751.90
34	$ 9,809.52	3.303241	$32,403.21
35	$10,300.66	3.001138	$30,913.71
36	$11,796.26	2.84454	$33,554.93
37	$12,072.71	2.712404	$32,746.07
38	$13,417.50	2.561809	$34,373.08
39	$15,014.39	2.457123	$36,892.20
40	$16,488.37	2.386295	$39,346.11
41	$17,578.53	2.243234	$39,432.76
42	$19,816.33	2.137938	$42,366.08
43	$20,064.41	2.056512	$41,262.70
44	$22,795.36	1.965713	$44,809.12
45	$25,440.98	1.895091	$48,212.98
46	$26,801.49	1.802233	$48,302.53
47	$27,536.23	1.786866	$49,203.55
48	$30,992.15	1.740161	$53,931.33
49	$34,893.01	1.673097	$58,379.40
50	$36,396.83	1.595089	$58,056.18
51	$36,936.43	1.507145	$55,668.58
52	$41,035.24	1.432187	$58,770.12
53	$42,533.74	1.356586	$57,700.69
54	$45,383.43	1.285498	$58,340.33
55	$50,034.62	1.255546	$62,820.74
56	$51,454.51	1.243079	$63,962.02
57	$55,140.29	1.213416	$66,908.14
58	$61,014.02	1.159513	$70,746.57
59	$64,329.16	1.118584	$71,957.57
60	$67,170.90	1.06943	$71,834.56
61	$73,383.51	1.023004	$75,071.63
62	$82,983.83	1	$82,983.83
Average of top 35 years			**$49,898.35**
Monthly Average			**$4,158.20**

Source: Social Security Administration

The table shows the wages earned in each year that this individual was working, indexed to compare with the current year's earnings. Then the top 35 indexed earnings years are totaled and divided by 420 to come up with the Average Indexed Monthly Earnings - your very own AIME. (Pure Prairie League had a song about Aimee, if you recall, in the 1970's.)

Notice the table begins at age 22 and ends at age 62. This is because the AIME is specifically based upon your current 40 earnings years and is calculated at age 62. Subsequent higher earnings in years beyond age 62 may eliminate the first years in the table.

With this table in mind, you can see how the AIME could increase if you continue working past age 62. Those earnings will be added to the table and if your earnings in the current year are greater than one of your lower earning years, the average would increase.

If you continue to work past age 62 and your earnings are not higher than the indexed earnings from past years, your AIME will not increase. However, even if you're not still working, it can be beneficial to delay receiving benefits after age 62 or even FRA, as this will increase the size of your benefit. We'll cover this later in Chapter 35 - Delayed Benefits.

For those of you who continue to work after FRA and receive benefits at the same time, if your earnings continue to increase your average your benefit will also increase. (*It's important to note that after age 62, additional earnings are added to the AIME calculation without being indexed. Your indexed earnings only include those prior to age 62, earnings thereafter are not indexed when used in the AIME calculation.)*

As you might guess, this AIME isn't the amount of retirement benefit you will receive: more factors need to be applied to come up with your Primary Insurance Amount (PIA), then your actual retirement age is applied to the PIA to calculate your benefit amount. But we're getting ahead of ourselves here. Let's find out what makes up the PIA.

4. Primary Insurance Amount (PIA)

The Primary Insurance Amount (PIA) is the projected amount of Social Security retirement benefits you will receive upon reaching Full Retirement Age - FRA, in Social Security Administration parlance.

The PIA is only one of the three main factors used in determining the actual amount of your retirement benefit - the other factors being your Full Retirement Age (FRA) and the date (or rather, your age relative to FRA) when you elect to begin receiving retirement benefits.

So how is the PIA calculated?

In true government style, this calculation can be pretty convoluted. You start off with your Average Indexed Monthly Earnings (AIME - which we defined in Chapter 3). Then, hold onto your hat, because it gets hairy from here (this calculation uses 2015 figures):

- the first $826 of your AIME is multiplied by 90%

- the amount between $826 and $4,980 is multiplied by 32%

- any amount in excess of $4,980 is multiplied by 15%

Note: these are the figures for 2015. The figures used (referred to as "bend points") are based upon the year when the retiree is first eligible to claim benefits - at age 62. See Chapter 5 for a further explanation of

Bend Points. For updated annual figures, you can find the updates posted on my blog each year as they become available: www.FinancialDucksInARow.com.

So let's work through a couple of examples:

Our first retiree will reach age 62 in 2015 and is hoping to begin taking Social Security benefits immediately upon eligibility - to get what's coming to her. Her AIME has been calculated as $6,500. Applying the formula, we get the following:

- first bend point: $743.40 ($826 * 90%)

- second bend point: $1,329.28 ($4,980 - $826 = $4,154 * 32%)

- excess: $228 ($6,500 - $4,980 = $1,520 * 15%)

- For a total PIA of: $2,300.60 ($743.40 + $1,329.28 + $228)

The second example retiree will also reach age 62 in 2015. His AIME has been calculated as $4,000. Applying the formula:

- first bend point: $743.40 (same as above)

- second bend point: $1,015.68 ($4,000 - $826 = $3,174 * 32%)

- excess: $0

- For a total PIA of: $1,759.00 ($743.40 + $1,015.68)

You should note the PIA is always rounded down to the next multiple of $0.10 - otherwise in the first example the PIA would have been $2,300.68 and the second would have been $1,759.08.

And that's just the start!

Once your PIA is calculated, it doesn't just sit there like the boring number it appears to be. Each year, if you're still working, your PIA will adjust according to the additional earnings you've received. And even if you're not working the PIA forms the basis of calculation of your actual benefit. Each year an annual Cost of Living Adjustment is applied as well as any additional (increased) earning years that may impact your AIME. The age you begin taking the payment of retirement benefits is factored into the equation as well, which you'll see in Chapter 6 – Calculating Your Retirement Benefit.

5. Bend Points

Caution – if math and calculations aren't of a great deal of interest to you, the following section may make you drowsy. Please proceed with caution, and try not to operate heavy machinery while reading this chapter.

Bend points (mentioned in the preceding chapter Primary Insurance Amount) are portions of your average income (Average Indexed Monthly Earnings - AIME) in specific dollar amounts indexed each year, based upon an obscure table called the Average Wage Index (AWI) Series. They're called bend points because they represent points on a graph of various levels of AIME with the points applied, resulting with the PIA (and the graph actually bends! See the chart on page 21.).

If you're interested in how Bend Points are used you can see Chapter 4 – Primary Insurance Amount, or PIA. However, in this chapter we'll go over how Bend Points are calculated each year. To understand this calculation you need to go back to 1979: the year of the Three Mile Island disaster, the introduction of the compact disc, and the Iranian hostage crisis. According to the AWI Series, in 1979 the Social Security Administration placed the AWI figure for 1977 at $9,779.44 - AWI figures are always two years in arrears, so for example, the AWI figure used to determine the 2015 bend points is from 2013.

With the AWI figure for 1977, it was determined the first bend point for 1979 would be set at $180, and the second bend point at $1,085. The reason behind the specific amounts is unknown to me, but it's safe to assume they are part of an indexing formula set up when the bend point concept was created. At any rate, now that we know these two numbers, we can jump back to 2013's AWI Series figure, which is $44,888.16. It all becomes a matter of a formula now:

The current year's AWI Series figure divided by 1977's AWI figure, times the bend points for 1979 equals the current year bend points.

So here is the math for 2015's bend points:

- $44,888.16 / $9,779.44 = 4.5901

- 4.5901 * $180 = $826.22, which is rounded down to $826 - the first bend point

- 4.5901 * $1,085 = $4,980.26, rounded to $4,980 - the second bend point

And that's all there is to it.

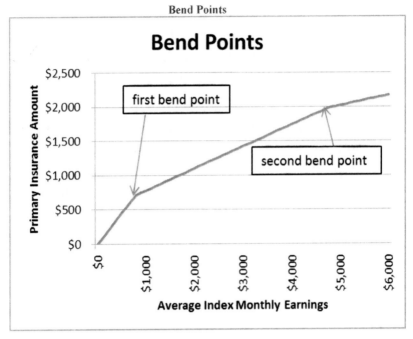

Source: Social Security Administration

As illustrated in the chart above, when your AIME increases the corresponding PIA and ultimately your benefit amount decreases in the percentage of income "replacement".

Why Bend Points?

We covered what bend points are and how they're applied, but we haven't discussed just why they exist at all. If you've been paying attention to all of the higher math going on earlier in this section you probably have a clue about it.

Bend points were put into place in order to ensure that folks at the lower end of the earnings spectrum receive a larger percentage of replacement income from the Social Security system, and as your lifetime income increases a smaller and smaller percentage is replaced by retirement benefits.

The income up to the first bend point is multiplied by 90%, ensuring a higher percentage of the first income amount is preserved. The income above the first bend point but less than the second bend point is multiplied by 32%; the amount above the second bend point is multiplied by a mere 15%.

Calculations

6. Calculating Your Retirement Benefit

As mentioned earlier, there are three factors that go into determining the Social Security retirement benefit amount: your PIA (Primary Insurance Amount), your FRA (Full Retirement Age), and the age you are when you start receiving benefits (your age relative to your FRA). We covered the PIA and the FRA earlier. Having these two numbers, we need to consider whether you are applying for early benefits which would result in a reduced benefit amount, or if you're delaying receipt of benefits to increase the amount.

Applying Early for Reduced Benefit Amount

When you apply early (before your FRA), a formula goes into effect to determine how much your benefit will be reduced. To perform this calculation, first you will determine how many months there are between your FRA and the age at which you'll start receiving benefits. Your PIA will be reduced by a percentage based upon the number of months you calculate. The first 36 months are multiplied by 5/9 of 1% (or 0.005556), and any months beyond 36 are multiplied by 5/12 of 1% (or 0.004167).

So if your FRA is age 66 and you intend to begin receiving benefits in the month you are age 62 years and 6 months, your PIA would be reduced by 20% for the first 36 months (36 * 5/9% = 20%) plus an

additional 2½% for the remaining 6 months (6 *
5/12% = 2½%) for a total of 22½% reduction.

> The maximum amount the PIA can be reduced is
> 25% for folks with FRA of age 66, ranging up to
> 30% for those with FRA of age 67.

When you come up with your reduction factor, apply
the factor to your PIA and the result is your Social
Security retirement benefit amount. You can see in
the table on the next page how waiting a few months
or years can make a big difference to your benefit
amount. This change can have a huge impact on your
lifetime benefits - because once you start receiving
your benefit it won't change other than with the
annual COLA (Cost of Living Adjustment) increases,
unless you continue to work while receiving benefits
which could increase your PIA. The other way to
increase your benefit is to take the "do over" -
described later in Chapter 31, although this method
has been altered recently and has much less effect.

Delaying Receipt of Benefits to Increase the Amount

If you are delaying your retirement beyond FRA,
you'll increase the amount of benefit you are eligible
to receive. This amount will be 8% per year for folks
born after 1942 (known as Delayed Retirement Credit
or DRC). The increase is for each year you delay
receiving benefits - which can be an increase of as

much as 32%. See the table for the increase amounts per year based upon birth year:

Maximum Factors Based on Age

Birth Year	FRA	Delay Credit (DRC)	Maximum (age 70)
1940	65 & 6 mos.	7%	131½%
1941	65 & 8 mos.	7½%	132½%
1942	65 & 10 mos.	7½%	131¼%
1943-1954	66	8%	132%
1955	66 & 2 mos.	8%	130⅔%
1956	66 & 4 mos.	8%	129⅓%
1957	66 & 6 mos.	8%	128%
1958	66 & 8 mos.	8%	126⅔%
1959	66 & 10 mos.	8%	125⅓%
1960 & later	67	8%	124%

Source: Social Security Administration

You can see the impact of delaying receipt of retirement benefits – you could receive a 57% higher benefit payment by delaying to age 70 versus starting benefits at age 62. *(Note: the 57% higher benefit is based on receiving a 75% benefit when filing early, versus an increased 132% benefit when filing later.)* Of course, by taking benefits later you're foregoing receipt of several years of monthly benefit payments; if you start taking benefits at the earliest age, for several years you'd be ahead in terms of total benefit received. This advantage tends to go away as you age, though. The break-even point is reached in your late 70's to early 80's in most cases, which we'll review a bit later.

7. Calculating the Spousal Benefit

The Spousal Benefit is one of the more confusing aspects of the Social Security retirement benefit system. It may be vaguely familiar to you that the spouse with the lower wage base is eligible for half of the higher wage base spouse's benefit, or something like that.

How is the Spousal Benefit actually calculated?

First of all, the Spousal Benefit is based upon a differential - between a percentage of your spouse's Primary Insurance Amount (PIA) and your own PIA.

So how does this work? Let's look at an example:

A husband and wife are the same age with a Full Retirement Age (FRA) of 66. The wife has a substantially lower wage base than the husband. At age 62 she files for the reduced benefit based on her own record, from a PIA of $800. Her benefit is reduced to $600 due to filing early.

Later on when they reach age 66 the husband files for benefits at his unreduced amount of $2,000 (equal to his PIA). The wife is now eligible for a Spousal Benefit since her husband has filed. The benefit is based on the differential between 50% of his PIA ($1,000) and her PIA ($800). The differential between those two factors is $200 ($1,000 minus $800). This amount is then added to her reduced benefit for a total benefit of $800 (COLAs have been eliminated from this example to keep it simple).

Let's adjust the example: Instead of drawing her own benefit as early as possible, the wife has waited until FRA to begin drawing her own benefit, at the same time as the husband. Now her Spousal Benefit will still be $200 (the differential between 50% of his PIA and her PIA), making her total benefit $1,000 (her unreduced benefit of $800 plus the $200 Spousal Benefit differential).

What if the wife is younger? As long as she's at least age 62 she can begin receiving the Spousal Benefit as soon as her husband applies for benefits. It's important to know though, if she decides to file for the Spousal Benefit prior to her FRA the Spousal Benefit factor is correspondingly reduced (as would be her own benefit if she filed early). Instead of 50% of her husband's PIA, at her age 62 the factor would be reduced to 35% of her husband's PIA and then the differential calculated as explained before. This reduction is calculated as 25/36ths of one percent (or 0.006944) for each month before her FRA, up to 36 months, plus 5/12ths of one percent (0.004167) for each month more than 36 before FRA. The reduction factor is then taken against the original 50% factor to determine the actual percentage of the husband's PIA that will be received.

Reduction Factors for Spousal Benefits, FRA 66		
Age wife files for Spousal Benefits	% of husband's PIA	Benefit if husband's PIA is $2,000
62	35.0%	$700
63	37.5%	$750
64	41.7%	$834
65	45.8%	$916

Source: Social Security Administration

Note: The roles could be reversed, with the husband taking the Spousal Benefit based upon his wife's record. Apologies for the gender specificity, it just becomes very clumsy to refer to the "lower earning spouse" and the "higher earning spouse".

And lastly, what if the wife has not filed for her own benefit? Again, as long as her husband has applied, she can file for the Spousal Benefit based upon his PIA. If she's at FRA there is no differential between her PIA (since she hasn't filed) and his factor-applied PIA, so the 50% factor is applied to his PIA and the result will be her Spousal Benefit - until she files for her own benefit. When she files for her own benefit the Spousal Benefit offset calculation will once again be based on the differential between the two PIA's. *(This action is known as a restricted application – more on this in Chapter 36.)*

If she hasn't filed and she's under FRA her own benefit <u>will automatically be filed for</u> when she files for Spousal Benefits, under a rule known as *deemed filing* (see Chapter 38 for details). Since she's younger than FRA when deemed filing applies there will still be a differential between her PIA and half of her spouse's PIA, and the reduced Spousal Benefit differential would be added to her early-filing-reduced benefit to provide the total benefit.

It is important to note if the spouse with the lower income files for retirement benefits before FRA and is eligible at that time for the Spousal Benefit (that is, the spouse with the higher income has also filed for benefits) deemed filing takes effect and both the retirement benefit AND the Spousal Benefit will be permanently reduced. This applies ONLY if the spouse is eligible for both benefits in the month he or she first applies for a retirement benefit prior to FRA. See Chapter 38 for more details and examples of Deemed Filing.

See Part 4, especially Chapters 33 through 40, for additional information about Spousal Benefit tactics for you to consider. We've only touched the most common basic examples thus far.

8. Calculating the Survivor Benefit

The Social Security system has provisions for taking care of the surviving spouses and dependents of workers who have earned credits under the system. There are two particular benefits you should be aware of - a small lump-sum death benefit of $255, and a Survivor Benefit based upon the worker's Primary Insurance Amount. It is the latter of these benefits which requires considerable review.

The Social Security Survivor Benefit

When a primary wage earner dies the Social Security system has a way to help care for the surviving spouse. The Survivor Benefit is often equal to the primary wage earner's retirement benefit (more on this in a moment), and this benefit replaces any other retirement benefits that the surviving spouse is receiving if they're less. You cannot receive a Survivor Benefit and a Spousal or regular retirement benefit at the same time.

The mechanics of the Social Security Survivor Benefit can apply to widows or widowers at various ages depending upon the circumstances, as well as to the children and/or parents of the primary worker if they are considered dependents of the primary worker. We'll cover each category in turn.

Widows and Widowers

When the primary wage earner dies the surviving spouse is entitled to receive a Survivor's Benefit based on the primary wage earner's retirement benefit. Of course, if the surviving spouse is currently receiving a retirement benefit based upon his or her own record and that retirement benefit is equal to or more than the Survivor Benefit, the surviving spouse will continue to receive his or her own retirement benefit.

Calculating the Survivor Benefit

Different rules apply depending upon whether or not the late spouse was already receiving benefits based on his or her own record, as well as the age of the surviving spouse when he or she begins receiving Survivor Benefits.

We'll look at the easy one first: when the late or decedent spouse was not already receiving benefits based on his or her own record.

When The Decedent Spouse Was Not Receiving Benefits

In the case where the late spouse has not already begun to receive benefits based upon his or her own record there are three factors you need to take into account: the age of the surviving widow(er), the age of the decedent at death, and the Primary Insurance Amount (PIA) of the decedent. PIA is the amount the late spouse would receive in benefits at his or her Full Retirement Age (FRA).

If the deceased was younger than or exactly at Full Retirement Age, then the PIA will be the benefit for our calculation. In the event the deceased was older than FRA, he or she would have accrued Delayed Retirement Credits (DRCs) which would have the effect of increasing the benefit amount the surviving widow(er) is eligible for. These credits are equal to 8% for each year (2/3% for each month) beyond FRA that the deceased spouse lived, up to age 70. Past age 70 there are no additional DRCs. See Chapter 6 for more on DRCs.

The last factor is the age at which the surviving spouse begins receiving the Survivor Benefits. These can begin as early as age 60, at which point the benefit will be reduced to 71.5% of the benefit determined in the paragraph above. Between age 60 and Full Retirement Age (of the surviving spouse) the amount of benefit increases pro-rata to eventually equal 100% of the deceased spouse's benefit (as determined above). There is no additional increase if the surviving spouse delays receipt of Survivor Benefits after FRA, although these benefits can begin at any age thereafter at 100%.

If the Decedent Spouse Was Already Receiving Benefits

This calculation is much more complicated. When the deceased is already receiving benefits we need to work through some additional calculations to determine the Survivor Benefit.

To start with, if the late spouse began his or her benefits at or after FRA, then the amount of benefit for our calculation is equal to the actual monthly benefit amount the deceased was receiving upon his or her death.

On the other hand, if the deceased had started receiving benefits prior to FRA, the amount of his or her benefit would be something less than his or her PIA. If that's the case the Social Security rules have determined the operative amount of benefit might be something more than the benefit the deceased was receiving upon his or her death.

Here's how it works: Three amounts are calculated –

1. The amount of benefit the decedent was actually receiving;

2. The amount equal to 82.5% of the PIA of the decedent; and

3. The reduced benefit based on the PIA of the decedent and the survivor's age (see the paragraph above "The Age of the Survivor" for details on this calculation).

These three amounts are listed from lowest to highest, and then the following determination is made: if #3 is less than either of the first two, that amount is used for the calculations. If #3 is the greatest of the three amounts, then the greater of the first two amounts is the benefit amount used for the calculations.

I realize the computation is very complex and convoluted, so here's a brief example:

Let's say Jane is the surviving spouse and her late husband Dick had started receiving his SS benefit earlier this year at age 62. Jane is now 64. Dick's PIA was $2,000, so when he started receiving his benefit at age 62 it was reduced to $1,500.

We run our calculations to come up with the three figures:

1. $1,500 (actual benefit Dick was receiving);

2. $1,650 (82.5% of Dick's PIA); and

3. the reduced benefit based upon Dick's PIA and Jane's age, which calculates to 90.167% times $2,000, or $1,803.

Arranging these figures from lowest to highest gives us 1, 2, 3. As described above, if #3 is the largest of the three figures then the larger of the first two is the actual benefit - so #2, $1,650, is the amount of the survivor benefit Jane is eligible for in these circumstances. This is the maximum amount of Survivor Benefit Jane is eligible to receive.

Reductions to the Survivor Benefit

If the surviving spouse elects to begin receiving survivor benefits before Full Retirement Age (FRA), the benefit is subject to actuarial reduction just the same as retirement benefits are reduced. Since a surviving spouse is eligible to begin receiving early benefits at age 60 (instead of age 62 for regular or Spousal Benefits), the "usual" age table is shifted by 2 years. Whereas FRA for regular or Spousal Benefits for those born between 1943 and 1954 is age 66, for a Survivor Benefit FRA is age 66 for those born between 1945 and 1956. (See Chapter 2 for the FRA ages and actuarial adjustments. Adjust the birth year by 2 for Survivor Benefit.) If the surviving spouse is disabled, early benefits may be received as early as age 50, with the actuarial reduction the same as if benefits begin at age 60 (no further reduction, in other words).

In addition to the benefit mentioned above, there is a Survivor Benefit available to a surviving spouse who is not yet age 60 or older if there are children under age 16 the surviving spouse is caring for, or a child of any age who has become disabled before age 22. This Survivor Benefit, known as a Parent's Benefit, is equal to 75% of the FRA benefit (PIA) of the deceased spouse - and this benefit lasts until the child reaches age 16. Additionally, each child under age 18 will also receive a Surviving Dependent's Benefit (more on this later) until age 18.

It should be noted there is no increase in benefits by delaying receipt of Survivor Benefits after FRA (same as the Spousal Benefit), so a widow or widower should generally begin taking Survivor Benefits no later than FRA. In addition, deemed filing (see Chapter 38) does not apply to Survivor Benefits.

It should also be noted a divorced spouse who survives a deceased worker is also eligible for the Survivor Benefit, as long as the couple was married for at least 10 years.

Children

Any child under age 18 (19 if attending school) who survives a deceased worker who has earned the maximum credits is eligible to receive a Survivor Benefit equal to 75% of the FRA benefit of the deceased parent.

If the child is disabled, the age limit does not apply – the disabled child of a deceased, eligible worker can continue to receive the Survivor Benefit for the remainder of his or her life. The disability must have begun prior to age 22.

In addition to the children of the deceased worker, this benefit can be available to step-children, grandchildren, step-grandchildren, or adopted children of the deceased worker, as long as the deceased worker provided 50% or more support to the child.

Surviving Parents Over Age 62

In the event the deceased worker had provided more than 50% of the support for an older parent (over age 62), the surviving parent will also be eligible to receive a Survivor Benefit. This Survivor Benefit is based on the age of the surviving parent, and actuarial reductions apply to these benefits if received before FRA of the survivor.

Family Maximum

For the whole family of the deceased wage earner, that is, surviving children under 18, spouse and parents, a maximum benefit amount applies - equal to between

150% and 180% of the deceased worker's basic benefit (specific calculations in Chapter 9).

Bear in mind, any Survivor Benefit received by a surviving divorced spouse does not count toward this family maximum.

9. Calculating the Family Maximum Benefit

When members of an eligible worker's family are receiving benefits based upon the worker's record, such as spousal benefits, benefits for children, or other family members' benefits, a maximum amount of benefit can be distributed in total. (There is a separate maximum benefit computation for disability benefits, which we'll cover in Chapter 15.)

How the Family Maximum Benefit is Computed

When computing the Family Maximum Benefit (FMax or FMB), the Social Security Administration falls back to its old habits of using a very convoluted formula, similar to the formula for computing the Primary Insurance Amount (PIA). The formula starts with the PIA, breaking it into four separate portions based upon Bend Points (and no, these are not the same Bend Points as those used in determining the retirement benefit).

If you don't want to follow the math behind the calculation of the Bend Points, you can go ahead and skip down to the last paragraph - there we talk about the actual computation for the current year.

The Bend Points for FMax are based upon when they were first calculated in 1979. At the time, the Average Wage Index (AWI) was $9,779.44 for 1977 (remember, the AWI is always two years behind) - and for 2013 the AWI is $44,888.16. Dividing the 2013 AWI by the 1977 AWI gives us a factor of 4.5901.

The original Bend Points for FMax were: $230, $332, and $433. Multiplying these Bend Points by our factor of 4.5901 gives us FMax Bend Points of $1,056, $1,524, and $1,987 for 2015. These are rounded to the nearest dollar.

Computation for the Current Year

So here's how we use those bend points to determine the FMax, for a worker who becomes age 62 or dies in 2015 before attaining age 62:

1. 150% of the first $1,056 of the PIA, plus

2. 272% of the amount between $1,056 and $1,524 of the PIA, plus

3. 134% of the amount between $1,524 and $1,987 of the PIA, plus

4. 175% of the amount above $1,987 of the PIA.

The total of the four amounts is then rounded to the next lower multiple of $.10 if it's not already a multiple of $.10.

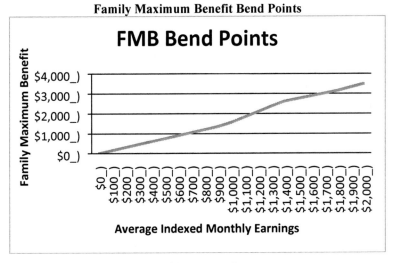

Source: Social Security Administration

Here's an example:

A worker age 62 with a PIA of $2,000 has a FMax calculated as follows:

1. 150% times $1,056 = $1,584

2. 272% times $468 ($1,524 minus $1,056) = $1,272.96

3. 134% times $463 ($1,987 minus $1,524) = $620.42

4. 175% times $13 ($2,000 minus $1,987) = $22.75

Adding these together ($1,584 + $1,272.96 + $620.42 + $22.75) equals $3,500.13, rounded down to a FMax of $3,500.10 for this particular worker in 2015.

10. The Impact of Zero Years

Remember when we talked about how your Social Security Benefit is calculated in Chapter 6? Your highest (indexed) 35 earning years during your career are put into a formula, then averaged by dividing the result by 420, the number of months in 35 years. And if you have less than 35 years of earnings, any missing years become zeros.

So, you can guess what might happen when you have years with zero earnings in your record. Naturally your average is going to be reduced (possibly quite dramatically) by any year(s) when you had zero earnings.

Let's say you have 35 years of earnings at the maximum amount, which will give you (for 2014) a FRA monthly benefit of $2,711. But if you only had 30 years at the maximum earnings amount and the remaining 5 years were zero earnings years, your benefit would be reduced to $2,531, an annual reduction of $2,160. Taking this further, if there were 15 "zero" years and all other years were at the maximum amount, your FRA benefit would be reduced to $2,106, for an annual reduction of $7,260.

This often occurs when an individual chooses to retire early, and/or has years in which he or she has not earned during his or her career, such as when raising children or going to school.

11. Making Every Month Count

Earlier, we covered the way your benefits increase when you delay your Social Security application, but did you realize that even delaying a few months can have a significant impact on your benefit? This is the case for all benefits, whether taking them before FRA or after, since your age is always calculated by the month. Increase or reduction factors are applied for each month of delay or early application, respectively.

Early Application Factors

For each month prior to your Full Retirement Age (FRA), a reduction factor is applied. For the 36 months just prior to your FRA, your benefit is reduced by 5/9 of 1% (0.005556) - so applying a full 36 months prior to FRA will result in a reduction of 20% (5/9% * 36 = 20%). Any months greater than 36 will result in a 5/12 of 1% reduction (0.004167), which means applying an additional year earlier will result in 5% more reduction, added to the 20%.

For each month after age 62 you delay applying for benefits, you'll increase the amount of your actual benefit - delaying to age 63 will eliminate 5% of the reduction versus applying at age 62. If your FRA is 66, delaying to age 64 will eliminate an additional 6.66% of reduction, as will delaying each additional year up to FRA. But the key is that even a few months' delay can increase your benefit. The amount of your benefit when you file is permanent, unless some other factor impacts it such as suspending or working while receiving benefits (more on these topics later).

Delayed Application Factors

When you delay applying for benefits past your FRA, you receive an increase in your benefit above your PIA. These increases are known as Delayed Retirement Credits, or DRCs. DRCs are better than the increase (or rather, lack of decrease) you achieve by delaying application after age 62. For each month you delay applying for benefits beyond FRA your benefit will increase by 2/3 of 1%, for a total increase each year of 8% (a little less for folks born prior to 1943).

So - make every month count! If you can delay even by a few months it can make a long-lasting difference in your lifetime benefits - and potentially for your spouse as well, if he or she survives you.

It should be noted that DRCs only accrue up to age 70. At age 70 your increase factors have maximized and no further factors will be applied. Of course, if you're still working and earning fat cash your benefit could possibly continue to increase beyond your age 70, but that's a topic for another time. Suffice it to say there is no additional DRC earned after you've reached age 70, so the latest age you should file for retirement benefits is age 70.

Disability Benefits

The foregoing sections (and the majority of this book) are focused primarily on Retirement Benefits. This section alone will point out some of the nuances for Disability Benefits.

12. Eligibility for Disability Benefits

As mentioned previously, there is a different set of rules regarding eligibility for Disability Benefits as opposed to Retirement Benefits. The minimum number of credits (quarters of work) is based upon your age, since it is very feasible you could become disabled early in your working career. The amount of benefits is correspondingly reduced by the number of years you may have been employed and earning credits.

There are two tests to determine eligibility for Disability Benefits:

- A "recent work" test, based upon your age at the time you became disabled; and

- A "duration of work" test to determine if, based upon your age, you have worked long enough under Social Security and have earned enough credits

If you become disabled before age 24 you need only 6 quarters (credits) during the three years before you become disabled in order to be eligible for disability benefits. And if you are between age 24 and 30 inclusive, you will need to have earned credits equal to half the time between age 21 and your current age in order to qualify. If you're age 31 or older you generally need to have earned more than 20 credits for eligibility.

The following table lists the recent work and duration of work credits required at various ages:

Recent Work and Duration of Work Credits

Disability at Age	Recent Work	During the Previous	Duration of Work
24 or younger	1½ years	3 years	1½
25	2	4	2
26	2½	5	2½
27	3	6	3
28	3½	7	3½
29	4	8	4
30	4 ½	9	4 ½
31 through 42	5	10	5
44	5	10	5½
46	5	10	6
48	5	10	6½
50	5	10	7
52	5	10	7½
54	5	10	8
56	5	10	8½
58	5	10	9
60	5	10	9½
62 or older	5	10	10

Source: Social Security Administration

To correctly use this table, consider if a person were to become disabled at age 44. This person would be eligible for Disability Benefits if he or she had worked a total of 5 out of the previous 10 years, and had earned 5½ years' worth of credits (22 credits). Likewise, if another individual became disabled at the age of 26, this person would become eligible for Disability Benefits if he or she has worked 2½ years out of the prior 5 years, and has earned 2½ years' worth of credits (10 credits).

You might be asking "How is it that the 44-year-old could work only 5 years out of the last 10 and still have 5½ years' worth of credits?" It's because the credits don't have to be within a specific number of recent years. The additional credits could have been earned more than 10 years ago.

13. When You've Stopped Working

When you leave full-time employment, there is a period of time when you will continue to be covered by Social Security for Disability Benefits.

Welcome to the 20/40 Rule.

The 20/40 Rule

If you have become disabled after you've left employment you may still be eligible for Disability Benefits - assuming you're under Full Retirement Age (FRA). In a case such as this, if you have worked the required number of quarters to be eligible for Disability Benefits, the rule is you must have worked 20 quarters out of the previous 40 quarters, earning at least the minimum.

The quarters don't need to be consecutive, but there must be 20 out of the 40 quarters prior to the onset of the disability. In other words, for five years after you leave employment you will be covered by Social Security for Disability Benefits, again assuming you're under FRA.

If you work, even part-time, ($1,220 earned in a quarter for 2015), this will count as a quarter for your coverage.

The 20/40 Rule is adjusted for age, as well. If you're under age 24 when you become disabled, you must have worked for 6 quarters out of the prior 12 quarters before you become disabled. Between ages

24 and 31, the numbers are half of the quarters after your age 21 - so if you're 29, you would need to have 16 of the 32 quarters after your age 21 (see the table in Chapter 12 for more details). After you reach age 31, the 20/40 Rule lives up to its name - 20 quarters out of the prior 40.

Once you reach FRA Disability Benefits are converted to Retirement Benefits so this rule doesn't need to be considered. We'll cover disability benefits upon retirement next.

14. Disability Benefits at Retirement

What options do you have when you've been receiving Social Security disability payments - and you're nearing Full Retirement Age (FRA)?

Disability Benefits at Retirement Age

When you reach FRA your Social Security Disability Benefit will automatically convert over to a Retirement Benefit at the same amount.

What does this mean? Essentially, once you reach FRA since you're now on a Retirement Benefit you have all of the features available to you as if you had not received any benefit prior to this point and you're now retired. So your spouse can collect Spousal Benefits based on your Primary Insurance Amount; Survivor Benefits are available; and you can choose to Suspend your benefits at FRA (no need to File before suspending, you have effectively filed when your Disability Benefit converted to Retirement Benefits). *(More on File and Suspend in Chapter 37.)*

By suspending you can earn Delayed Retirement Credits (DRCs) of 8% per year up to age 70, which will permanently increase your own benefit and your spouse's potential future Survivor Benefit.

Obviously, there is no requirement for you to change anything at all once you reach FRA - you can continue receiving the Retirement Benefit the same as you have been receiving the Disability Benefit up to this point.

It's an unusual situation, understandably, but something to keep in mind if you happen to be facing the circumstance of possibly suspending retirement benefits.

15. Family Maximum Benefit for Disability

Earlier we talked about the Social Security Family Maximum Benefit for a retired worker - and we mentioned there was a separate calculation for the Social Security Family Maximum Benefit (FMax or FMB) for a disabled worker.

This calculation is much simpler than the retired worker calculation for Family Maximum Benefits. But hang onto your hat, keep your arms and legs inside the car at all times, cuz this may get a little outtahand:

The family maximum for the spouse and children of a disabled worker is 85% of the worker's Average Indexed Monthly Earnings (AIME), but not less than the worker's Primary Insurance Amount (PIA) nor more than 150% of the PIA.

Example

Let's use the AIME amount from an earlier example where we explained how it's calculated: $4,000. For this worker in 2015, the PIA would be $1,759.

So, the maximum family benefit for the disabled worker's family would be equal to the lesser of 85% of the AIME or 150% of the PIA, but not less than the PIA.

- 85% of the AIME: 85% times $4,000 = $3,400

- 150% of the PIA: 150% times $1,759= $2,638.50

The rule is that the FMax is 85% of the AIME, but not greater than 150% of the PIA nor less than 100% of the PIA. Therefore in this case the maximum family benefit is $2,638.50, exactly 150% of the PIA.

Part 2: Reductions

Earnings Reductions

16. Earnings Tests

As we have discussed, you can receive Social Security benefits and continue working. If you happen to be younger than Full Retirement Age (FRA) and you earn more than certain amounts, your benefit will be reduced.

Note: these reductions are not really lost, your benefit will be increased at FRA to account for those benefits withheld due to earlier earnings.

<u>Earnings Tests</u>

If you're at or older than FRA when you begin receiving benefits, you may earn as much as you like and your benefit will not be reduced. However if you are younger than FRA your benefit will be reduced $1 for every $2 you earn over $15,720 before the year of FRA. In the year of FRA your benefit will be reduced by $1 for every $3 you earn over $41,880, up until the month you reach FRA. (2015 figures)

For example, let's say your benefit is $700 per month ($8,400 for the year) and you are age 63. You work and earn $20,000 during the year, which is $4,280 more than the earnings test for your age. The Social Security Administration would withhold a total of $2,140 from your benefit ($1 for every $2 over the limit). This is done by withholding the benefit for four months at the beginning of the following year, January through April - for a total of $2,800 being withheld. Beginning in May you'll receive your full $700 benefit, and in January of the following year you'll receive $660 extra for the additional amount withheld above the $2,140.

17. The year you begin benefits

As we discussed in the previous chapter, there are limits to the amount you can earn while receiving Social Security benefits.

What we haven't covered yet is just how these earnings impact your benefits in the year you first begin receiving your Social Security benefits. Here's how it works:

Prior to starting your benefits, no matter when you start them, you can earn as much as you like. The earnings limits only apply AFTER you've begun receiving your benefits. In the case of the years prior to FRA your benefit will be reduced when your monthly income is greater than $1,310 per month, for every month you are receiving Social Security benefits. This is just a pro-rated application of the annual limit of $15,720 for 2015.

The same pro-rate method is applied for the year of FRA - the monthly limit is $3,490 for 2015.

18. Earnings Test is Specific to the Individual

Another area we haven't covered is the concept of your household income versus the individual. This is best explained by an example, which is illustrated below:

In this example, the wife is 62 and she works a part-time job earning around $23,000 per year. She is planning to retire in June, and so her total earnings for the year will be approximately $11,500. She would like to begin taking Social Security benefits right after her retirement.

The question is this: will her earnings test be based upon her "individual" earnings, or on the higher combined earnings of the couple (husband is still working, earning in excess of the earnings test amount)? Since her earnings of approximately $11,500 are under the $15,720 earnings limit, her benefit would not be reduced - but if the earnings test is based upon both the husband and wife's earnings combined, her benefit would definitely be reduced. How does this work?

Each person's earnings record is specific to the individual - the only time the spouse's income enters into the equation is in calculating spousal or survivor's benefits. Therefore, the only earnings considered for the "earnings test" for the wife in our example - are hers and not the household (not including the husband's income, in other words).

One other time the household earnings are considered is when you file your tax return (see Chapter 23).

In addition, a special rule applies to the first year of retirement, when a person retires mid-year: the retiree who retires in mid-year is eligible for a full benefit (however reduced by age, in our example wife's case since she filed before FRA) for any whole month the person is considered retired and earning less than the monthly amount, regardless of total yearly earnings.

"Considered retired" when at less than Full Retirement Age is defined as having earned $1,310 or less per month and not performing substantial services in self-employment.

"Substantial services in self-employment" is defined as more than 45 hours per month in a business or more than 15 hours in a business in a highly skilled occupation (e.g., brain surgery or writing a book about Social Security).

With this in mind, the wife in our example would be eligible for her age-reduced benefit for the remainder of the year after her retirement, with no reductions due to earnings tests (as long as she doesn't pick up another job).

19. Payback When You've Earned Too Much

As explained in Chapter 16, when you've earned more than the annual limit, a portion of your benefit is withheld. However, there is an eventual "payback": when you reach FRA your reduced benefit is recalculated eliminating those months when your benefit was withheld, boosting your benefit for the future.

There's a misconception that you actually receive back the dollars withheld due to your over-earning. That's not exactly how it works - you actually get credit for the months when your benefit was withheld. This is much the same as how the "do-over" option works (details in Chapter 31), except you're not paying it back to the SSA, they're just never giving it to you.

For example, let's say you took your benefit at age 62 (reducing the benefit to 75% of your PIA) and you had earnings causing the SSA to withhold four months' worth of benefit each year for the four years between age 62 and 66. When you reach FRA you would actually improve your benefit by 7.22% - because your reduction would be adjusted to 82.22% of your PIA.

The increase is because you did not receive benefits for 16 months during the period between age 62 and 66 (4 months each year when they withheld your benefit), which equates to a 7.22% increase in benefits when multiplied by the reduction factors explained earlier: 5/12% for 12 months and 5/9% for 4 months, or 7.22%.

GPO and WEP

20. Windfall Elimination Provision

If you have worked in a job where your pay was subject to Social Security tax withholding, and you have also worked in a job where Social Security tax has not been withheld, such as for a government agency or an employer in another country, any pension you receive from the non-Social Security taxed job(s) may cause a reduction in your Social Security benefits. This reduction is known as the Windfall Elimination Provision (WEP). This provision was put in place to eliminate the "windfall" this sort of worker would otherwise receive. Without the WEP the worker is effectively double-dipping by receiving full benefits from both plans.

This provision primarily affects Social Security benefits when you have earned a pension in any job where you did not pay Social Security tax and you also worked in other jobs long enough to qualify for Social Security benefits. However, federal service where Social Security taxes are withheld (Federal Employees' Retirement System) will not reduce your Social Security benefits. The WEP may apply if:

- you reached age 62 after 1984; or

- you became disabled after 1985; and

- you first became eligible for a monthly pension for work on which you did not pay Social

Security taxes after 1985, even if you are still working.

Here's How It Works

True to form, the Social Security Administration doesn't make it easy to figure all this out.

You start out by determining your Primary Insurance Amount (PIA), which begins with your Average Indexed Monthly Earnings (AIME), and then take the Bend Points for your eligibility year (age 62) into account. For 2015, the first Bend Point is $826 and the second Bend Point is $4,980. As we discussed in Chapter 4 on Primary Insurance Amount (PIA), the amount of your AIME making up the first Bend Point is multiplied by 90%; the amount between the first Bend Point and the second Bend Point is multiplied by 32%; and finally any amount above the second Bend Point is multiplied by 15%. These three figures are added up to create your PIA.

However - if the WEP applies to your situation and you reached age 62 after 1989, the 90% factor (applied to the first Bend Point) can be reduced to as little as 40%. Effectively, this reduces the PIA for those folks affected by WEP by as much as $413 per month (for 2015). Since your PIA is being reduced, this can also reduce Spousal Benefits that are based on your PIA.

Exceptions

Adding to the complexity, the SSA has exceptions to the rule. If you worked for 30 years or more in the

Social Security taxed job and you earned "substantial" wages (substantial is defined as $22,050 for 2015 and is indexed annually), your 90% factor is not reduced at all. If you had substantial earnings for at least 21 years but less than 30 years, the 90% factor is reduced by 5% each year less than 30 years that you had "substantial" earnings in the Social Security-taxed job, with the lowest factor being 40%.

Additionally, the WEP doesn't apply to Survivor's benefits (but the Government Pension Offset does).

Other exceptions include the following:

- You are a federal worker first hired after December 31, 1983;

- You were employed on December 31, 1983 by a nonprofit organization which did not withhold Social Security taxes from your pay at first, but then began withholding Social Security taxes from your pay;

- Your only pension is based on railroad employment; or

- The only work you did for which you did not pay Social Security taxes was before 1957.

Limit on WEP Impact

There is a limit to the WEP reduction amount: no matter what your factor has been reduced to (from the original 90%), the resulting reduction cannot be more than 50% of your pension based on earnings after 1956 on which you did not pay Social Security taxes.

And lastly, the WEP also applies to Social Security Disability Benefits, using the same factors.

21. Government Pension Offset

A somewhat confusing situation occurs when a spouse is receiving either a Spousal Benefit or a Survivor's Benefit from Social Security while also receiving a pension from a federal, state, or local government. The Government Pension Offset (GPO) applies if the pension being received is from a job where Social Security taxes (Old Age, Survivor's and Disability Income, or OASDI) were not withheld.

The Social Security Administration will reduce the Spousal or Survivor's Benefit by a factor equal to two-thirds of the government pension he or she is receiving. This is called the Government Pension Offset, or GPO. Those are the facts of the situation. Now let's look at "Why"?

Why?

Eligibility for Spousal or Survivor's Benefits is based in part upon your own record with the Social Security administration. If your own current benefit is greater than the Survivor's or Spousal Benefit, of course you would not be receiving the Survivor's or Spousal Benefit - you can only receive either your own benefit or the Survivor's or Spousal Benefit, whichever is greater.

Since you are receiving a pension from a government job which did not require you to have Social Security tax withheld, your own Social Security record doesn't reflect the income earned from the job. The pension is designed to take the place of Social Security benefits - at least to some degree. This particular quandary was first addressed in 1977 with the amendments to the Social Security Act - but it really went too far at that stage.

1977 Amendment

Government pensions from jobs not subject to Social Security tax withholding are designed to be partially pension and partially compensation to replace Social Security benefits for the retiree. In 1977 an amendment was made to the Social Security Act to address the fact that, otherwise, a Spousal Benefit or Survivor's Benefit would be compensating the Spouse more than the system originally intended. The 1977 Amendment offset the Social Security Spousal or Survivor's Benefit dollar-for-dollar for the amount of pension received from government work which was not subject to Social Security tax (from a job the Spouse or Survivor worked).

1983 Amendment

In the 1983 Amendment, the GPO was improved for Spousal and Survivor's Benefits. Instead of the original dollar-for-dollar offset, now the Social Security Spousal or Survivor's Benefit is only reduced by two-thirds of the government pension. This more accurately reflects the fact that the government pension is part pension and part compensation to replace the Social Security benefit.

When Does the GPO NOT Apply?

It's possible your Spousal or Survivor's Benefit may not be impacted by the Government Pension Offset. Listed below are several situations in which the GPO does not apply:

- If you are receiving a government pension that is not based on earnings;

- If you are a state or local employee whose government pension is based on a job where you were paying Social Security taxes

  o on the last day of your employment and your last day was prior to July 1, 2004; or

  o during the last five years of employment and your last day of employment was July 1, 2004 or later. Depending on the circumstances, fewer than five years could be required for folks whose last day of employment falls between July 1, 2004 and March 1, 2009 inclusive.

- If you are a federal employee, including a Civil Service Offset employee, who pays Social Security taxes on your earnings. (A Civil Service Offset employee is a federal employee who was rehired after December 31, 1983, following a break in service of more than 365 days and had five years of prior civil service retirement system coverage);

- If you are a federal employee who elected to switch from the Civil Service Retirement System (CSRS) to the Federal Employees' Retirement System (FERS) on or before June 30, 1988. If you switched after that date, including during the open season from July 1, 1998 through December 31, 1998, you need five years under FERS to be exempt from the GPO;

- If you received or were eligible to receive a government pension before December 1982 and meet all the requirements for Social Security Spousal Benefits or Survivor's Benefits in effect in January 1977; or

- If you received or were eligible to receive a federal, state, or local government pension before July 1, 1983 and were receiving at least one-half support from your spouse.

22. When GPO and WEP Apply

These two rules within the Social Security Administration's procedures reflect reductions to Social Security benefits for receiving pension benefits from a job where your salary is not subject to Social Security withholding. Usually these are federal, state, or local government jobs, including teaching jobs at public institutions. The WEP applies to your own Social Security retirement benefit, while the GPO applies to your benefit as a spouse or survivor.

The WEP may impact you if you are receiving a pension from a non-covered government job and you also are qualified to receive Social Security benefits based upon your own record. Survivor's Benefits and Spousal Benefits are NOT subject to the WEP. For 2015 the maximum WEP reduction is $413 per month, but it can be much less (even eliminated) depending on how long you worked in the Social Security-covered job and how much money you made there (see Chapter 20 for more details).

The GPO may impact you if you are receiving a pension from a government job and are qualified to receive Spousal or Survivor's Benefits based upon your spouse's or ex-spouse's record. Your benefit may be reduced by an amount equal to two-thirds of the amount of your pension.

Taxes

23. How Social Security Benefits Are Taxed

You probably are aware a portion of your Social Security retirement benefit may be taxed. Do you know how the tax is calculated? Or how the taxable portion of your benefit is determined?

The Rules

A couple of different levels of income determine how much of your Social Security Benefit is taxed. The first level is $32,000 for a married couple filing jointly (MFJ) or $25,000 for single, head of household, or qualifying widow(er) filing statuses. If your Modified Adjusted Gross Income (MAGI) plus half of your Social Security benefit is less than this first level for your filing status, none of your Social Security benefit is taxable. *For the purpose of this calculation, MAGI includes tax exempt interest income.*

The second level is $44,000 for MFJ or $34,000 for the other filing statuses. If your MAGI plus half of your Social Security benefit is greater than the first level but less than the second level, as much as 50% of your Social Security benefit may be included in your taxable income.

If your MAGI is above the second level, as much as 85% of your Social Security benefit may be included in your taxable income.

Like most calculations in the tax code or where Social Security is involved, it's a mess to understand. I'll give you some examples below to illustrate how this works.

Examples

Here are a few examples:

Example 1. Married Filing Jointly, MAGI = $15,000; SS = $15,000:

1. MAGI	$15,000
2. Half of SS Benefit	$7,500
3. Provisional Income (PI) line 1 plus line 2	$22,500
4. First Level	$32,000
5. Subtract line 4 from 3 - if less than zero, enter zero and stop. No tax on SS Benefit	$0

Since the PI is less than the First Level, none of the SS benefit is taxed.

Example 2. Married Filing Jointly, MAGI = $25,000; SS = $20,000:

1. MAGI	$25,000
2. Half of SS Benefit	$10,000
3. Provisional Income (PI) line 1 plus line 2	$35,000
4. First Level	$32,000
5. Subtract line 4 from line 3	$3,000
6. Multiply 50% Level by .5	$1,500
7. Second Level	$44,000
8. Subtract line 7 from line 5 - if less than zero, enter zero and stop. Line 6 is added to your income as taxable	$0

Since the 50% level amount is greater than zero, half of the amount above the 50% level will be added to the taxable income for the couple. None of the benefit is includable at the 85% rate.

Example 3. Married Filing Jointly; MAGI = $45,000; SS = $20,000:

1. MAGI	$45,000
2. Half of SS Benefit	$10,000
3. Provisional Income (PI) line 1 plus line 2	$55,000
4. First Level	$32,000
5. Subtract 1st from PI (50% level)	$23,000
6. Multiply 50% Level by .5 - if more than $6,000, enter $6,000	$6,000
7. Second Level	$44,000
8. Subtract line 7 from line 3	$11,000
9. Multiply line 8 by .85	$9,350
10. Add line 6 and line 9	$15,350
11. Multiply line 2 by 1.70	$17,000
12. Lesser of line 10 or line 11 is added to your income as taxable	$15,350

Since the SS benefit was greater than the upper limit, a portion of the benefit is included at the 50% rate, and another portion is included at the 85% rate, for a total addition of $15,350 to taxable income for the couple.

Eventually all of the SS benefit is taxed at the 85% rate, when line 10 is less than line 11 in the table above.

Example 4. Married Filing Jointly; MAGI = $55,000;
SS = $20,000:

1. MAGI	$55,000
2. Half of SS Benefit	$10,000
3. Provisional Income (PI) line 1 plus line 2	$65,000
4. First Level	$32,000
5. Subtract 1st from PI (50% level)	$33,000
6. Multiply 50% Level by .5 - if more than $6,000, enter $6,000	$6,000
7. Second Level	$44,000
8. Subtract line 7 from line 3	$21,000
9. Multiply line 8 by .85	$17,850
10. Add line 6 and line 9	$23,850
11. Multiply line 2 by 1.70	$17,000
12. Lesser of line 10 or line 11 is added to your income as taxable	$17,000

Since the PI was greater than the 85% level, we did the same type of calculation as in Example 3, except this time the total of the 50% taxed amount and the 85% taxed amount was greater than 85% of the overall SS benefit, so only 85% of the benefit is added to the taxable income for the couple.

Hopefully these examples will help you to better understand how the amount of taxable Social Security benefit is calculated for various situations.

Part 3: The Administration

24. Talking to the Social Security Administration

I often recommend talking to the Social Security Administration (SSA), either at your local office or on their hotline, to review your particular situation. But this advice comes with a caveat: you need to know as much as you can about your options and what you are entitled to do so you are well-informed about what your options are when you speak with the SSA.

This is because the SSA representatives' default advice is often to recommend the option which provides you the largest benefit <u>today</u>. The reason for this may be because it is in the SSA's best interest for you to make your move now rather than later. This is because up to age 70 any delay results in an increase in your lifetime benefit, provided you live beyond age 80 (or so).

However, it is more likely that the default advice is geared toward the highest benefit today because a very high percentage of the eligible benefit recipients do not wish to delay receiving their benefit - so the folks you talk to at the SSA office are playing the averages by assuming that's what you want to do.

It is for these reasons it makes very good sense to know as much as possible about your situation and the options you have available (what you are entitled to) before you talk to the SSA. Explain to the representative what you're planning to do and have the representative run the numbers to tell you what your benefits will be in the scenario(s) you're suggesting.

It pays to be informed - and this is especially true when it's something as confusing and complicated (with so much potential gain and loss) as your Social Security benefits.

25. Checking Your Social Security Benefit

Historically, each of us used to receive an annual update of our benefit in the form of a statement. Beginning in 2011, this statement was no longer being printed and sent by mail automatically. However, as of September 2014, the decision was made to resume sending these paper statements, but only one every five years between the age of 25 and 60. Regardless of what the current status of the paper statement may be there is a way to get your statement online so you can see your information at any time.

It's quite simple to check out your up-to-date benefit projection in the Social Security system - at least the retirement estimates. Simply go to the Social Security website (www.SocialSecurity.gov/myaccount/) and register. Once you've done so you will be able to view your Social Security Statement.

Note: my colleague Andy Tilp pointed out an interesting fact. If you have your credit "frozen" at the credit bureaus, you will not be able to set up your account at Social Security online. I believe the answer to this dilemma is to temporarily "unfreeze" your credit, set up your account at Social Security, and then you can re-freeze your credit.

This statement that you receive online is identical to the statement you receive in the mail and you can rely on the figures there to help you with your planning activities. In the next chapter we'll review the statement itself.

I must say – I poke fun at the SSA on a regular basis (it's just so *easy!*), but I think they've done a pretty good job with their website. The site is relatively user-friendly, and there are useful tools there for performing calculations based on your records. It's worth the time investment to check it out!

26. Your Social Security Benefit Statement

In Chapter 25, we talked about how to get a Retirement Estimate from the Social Security website. This used to be mailed to you just prior to your birthday each year, but automatic mailings have been changed to once every five years. You can get a copy from the Social Security website at any time. It's important to understand just what this statement is telling you.

First Page

This page is your basic SSA boilerplate, explaining to you some of the current details of the Social Security system - for example, they're now explaining that the SSA system will, if no changes are made, have to reduce all benefits to 77% of scheduled benefits as of 2033, due to exhaustion of the Trust Fund.

Second Page

Now we're into the meat of the report. At the top of the page is the detail of your Estimated Benefits. These estimates assume your current earnings rates continue until the projected ages in the list. First are your Retirement Benefits – at Full Retirement Age (your FRA will be listed), at age 70, and at your early retirement age of 62. These figures are especially helpful when planning retirement income, assuming you expect to continue earning at your current income level until the projected age(s) and you further expect the Social Security system will continue to pay out to folks at your particular level of income in the future.

Next comes the section on Disability Benefits for you. This shows the amount of Social Security Disability Benefit you are currently eligible to receive.

The next section is for Family and Survivor's Benefits - indicating the amount of benefit your Child and/or your Surviving Spouse caring for your child under age 16 or who has reached Full Retirement Age would receive upon your death. Your spouse's Survivor Benefit is listed third – this is the amount payable to your Spouse after your death when he or she reaches Full Retirement Age. (*FYI: this figure is a very good approximation of your PIA if your earnings stopped as of the last reported year. This can be helpful for planning if you were to retire from regular employment and delay filing for benefits until a later date.*) Lastly, your Family Maximum Benefit (FMax) amount will be listed here as well.

The last portion in this top section is the information about whether you have earned enough credits to qualify for Medicare at age 65, followed by your birthdate and the most recent income estimate Social Security is basing their projected estimates of your benefit upon.

The bottom portion of the second page details how the benefits are estimated, including information about quarter-credits, assumptions made by the report, as well as the WEP and GPO calculations, and where they might apply.

Third Page

The Third Page of the statement lists out the details of your earnings record. This section is important to review carefully. You should review the earnings listed for each year and compare against your tax records or W2 statements to make sure the information the SSA has is correct. In addition to reviewing for correctness, you should look over your record and note the "zero" earnings years, as well as years when you earned considerably less than what you earned (or are earning) in later years.

As we've covered in other chapters, your benefits are based upon your 35 highest earning years, and so if you have had some "zero" years in the past or some very low earnings years, you can expect for your estimated benefit to reflect any increases the current year's income represents over your earlier low earnings or zero years. This only becomes significant once you have a full 35 year record in the system.

Another key here is your projected benefits listed on page 2 are based upon your earnings *remaining the same as your last reported year until your projected retirement age(s)*. If you choose, for example, to retire at age 55 and have no earnings subject to Social Security withholding, your projected benefit will be reduced since those years projected at your current earning level will actually be "zero" years. This reduction is in addition to any actuarial reductions you would experience by beginning to take retirement benefits before FRA.

In addition, if you have gaps showing in your earnings history you may have had a job which was not covered by Social Security, so you will be interested in knowing how the Windfall Elimination Provision (WEP) and/or the Government Pension Offset (GPO) may affect your benefits. See Chapters 20-22 for more details on WEP and GPO.

The middle portion of the Third Page shows how much you have paid into the system over the years - both the Social Security system and Medicare system, and it can be an eye-opener. Quite often we don't realize how the money we've paid in can stack up!

Lastly on the Third Page there are details about how to report any inaccuracies you might happen to find with your statement. It's much easier to resolve things early in the process rather than later - when you're possibly under the gun about applying for your benefits.

The Back Page

The Back Page of the statement is full of additional information about the Social Security system, benefit calculations, and other fun facts about your benefits. There are also details on how to find more information about your benefits as well.

I suggest you do get this statement from time to time, annually as you near retirement age, to ensure the records the SSA has for your past earnings are accurate and complete.

27. How COLAs Are Calculated

As you are probably aware, each year your Social Security benefits can be increased by a factor which helps to keep up with the rate of inflation - so your benefit's purchasing power doesn't decrease over time. These are called Cost Of Living Adjustments, COLAs for short. As of this writing, the most recent increase was for 2015, an increase of 1.7%. But how are these adjustments to your benefits calculated?

Calculating the COLA

There is an index, compiled and managed by the Bureau of Labor Statistics, called the Consumer Price Index for Urban Wage Earners and Clerical Workers, or CPI-W. Changes to the index measure the fluctuations in those prices over time. Each October, SSA looks at the CPI-W level for the third quarter of the year (averaging July, August and September), and compares it to the same level for the previous year's third quarter. The percentage of increase, if any, is then used as COLA for Social Security benefits. This is an automatic process; no action is required by Congress to enact the increases over time.

As an example, the CPI-W average for the third quarter of 2014 was 234.242, and for the same period in 2013 the average was 230.327.

When you compare the two, you come up with an increase of 1.699%, rounded to 1.7% - which is what the COLA was for 2015.

How it's applied

Simple enough, right? We have the COLA, just multiply it by your benefit, right? Not so fast there, calculator-breath. Staying true to form, SSA has a more complicated method to determine what your benefit will be each year. (Spoiler alert: the result is the same nonetheless.)

As we mentioned before in Chapter 6 on Calculating the Social Security Retirement Benefit, <u>when</u> you apply for benefits affects your benefit permanently. All benefit calculations begin with your Primary Insurance Amount (PIA), and are adjusted up or down depending on whether you applied for benefits after or before Full Retirement Age (FRA), correspondingly.

For example, if your Full Retirement Age is 66 and your PIA is $2,000 and you've filed for benefits at age 62 your actual benefit amount began at 75% of the PIA or $1,500. The COLA is applied to your PIA, after which your reduction is applied. So for a COLA of 3%, your new benefit amount would be $1,545 - calculated as PIA ($2,000) times COLA (3%) equals $2,060, times the reduction amount of 75%, for a total of $1,545.

Similarly, if you delayed your benefit to age 70, your benefit would begin at 132% of your PIA, or $2,640.

For our example increase of 3%, your new benefit would be $2,719. Amounts are always rounded down to the next lower dollar. In this case, your PIA would have already had the earlier years' COLAs applied (assuming there were COLAs).

28. Withholding for Your Social Security

Many folks find upon filing their income tax return that a portion of their Social Security benefits are taxable – often a significant portion, up to 85%. It's also often a surprise that since the benefit is taxable there hasn't been enough tax withheld from other sources throughout the year - which not only requires you to pay up come April 15, but it can also cause a penalty for underpayment of tax to be applied. This underpayment penalty is most likely if the amount of underpayment is $1,000 or more.

There are many ways to deal with this situation - it's not required for you to withhold tax from each and every source of income. As long as you have enough tax withheld or timely estimated payments are made, it doesn't matter the source of the money paid in. Listed below are four withholding methods you might use to help make sure you don't have an underpayment penalty.

Withholding Methods

Estimated Tax Payments. This method isn't actually withholding, but it achieves the same purpose. On April 15, June 15, September 15 and January 15, payments are made to the IRS. In addition, any overpayments you made in the previous year can be applied in place of any portion of the estimated payments you've calculated. It's important that the estimated payments be made in relatively equal portions throughout the year, otherwise you may still be subject to an underpayment (or late payment) penalty. If your income from all of your sources varies through the year, your estimated payments should be in proportion with the income, net of deductions for the period.

Withholding From an IRA Distribution. This method is a little-known way to deal with meeting the withholding requirements. Essentially, when you take a distribution from your IRA (or Qualified Retirement Plan such as a 401(k) plan), you have the option to have the custodian withhold taxes and submit them to the IRS. No matter if you take a single distribution or quarterly or monthly distributions, the withholding is counted as evenly withheld throughout the year - taking timeliness of the distribution and withholding out of the picture.

Withholding From Your Other Income. You probably already know this, but you can have tax withheld from many other sources of income. Pensions, annuities, part-time work and the like can all be set up with tax being withheld throughout the year. This is accomplished by filling out a W-4 for a job, or W-4P for pensions - you can set the amount of withholding to literally any amount which makes sense for your situation.

Withholding From Your Social Security Benefit. Much the same as your other income, you can set up your Social Security payments to have tax withheld from each payment. This is accomplished by filling out a

Form W-4V, and selecting the percentage of your monthly benefit you'd like to have withheld - you can choose from 7%, 10%, 15% or 25% to be withheld. You can find Form W-4V at the IRS website or by calling 800-829-3676.

How much should you have withheld? Of course, the answer is going to be different for each person. It's determined by how much tax you are assessed, how much withholding you have from other sources, and the shortfall in withheld (or estimated payment) tax. If your underpayment when you file your return is greater than $1,000 you may be assessed a penalty for underpayment of tax.

Part 4: Tips and Strategies

29. Retiring Early

In prior chapters we discussed how beneficial it can be to delay receiving Social Security benefits as long as you can. If you'll recall, as long as you aren't in dire need of the money for living expenses, it makes good financial sense to delay receiving your benefit to age 70 in many cases, but of course not all.

Social Security is such a great benefit because this government-backed income stream is pretty much as good of a longevity insurance policy as you can get. When you start receiving the benefit you'll continue to receive it throughout your entire life - at least under current law, and it's doubtful politicians will have the stomach to change that fact. The reason you should delay receiving your benefit as long as possible is due to the fact that <u>when</u> you start receiving your benefit impacts the amount you will receive for your entire life - plus, depending upon the amount of your spouse's benefit, it could impact the amount your spouse would receive as a Survivor's Benefit as well.

But there are times when it may make more sense to begin receiving your benefit earlier.

Starting Early

Circumstances require it. If you're in ill health, have a shortened life expectancy, or have very limited other resources, it may be necessary to start taking your Social Security benefit early. The financial calculations we do to illustrate how delaying receipt of benefits is the better choice quite often assume the recipient will live to at least age 80 or beyond and can get along using other resources until age 70. If one or the other (or both) of these circumstances is not the case for you, it likely makes more sense to begin taking your benefit earlier.

Bear in mind that filing early impacts your spouse's potential Survivor Benefit and as such even if you have a shortened life expectancy it might be better for your family in the long run to delay filing to increase future benefits.

Spouse with a relatively small benefit. If the spouse with the lower wage base has earned a relatively small benefit and intends to switch over to a Spousal Benefit as soon as it makes financial sense (may require a File and Suspend by the other spouse), it might make sense to start taking the smaller retirement benefit early even though it is reduced. In this case the financial impact of starting to take the benefit early doesn't amount to a significant reduction in real dollars so taking the benefit for several years is just extra "gravy on your french fries" in a manner of speaking.

For example, Dick and Jane are both 62 years old with Full Retirement Age(s) of 66 and Dick's PIA (Primary Insurance Amount) is $400 per month, while Jane's PIA is $2,000. If Dick takes his own retirement benefit at age 62 he is giving up 25% of his benefit, but in real dollars it only amounts to $100 per month. In this circumstance the actual amount of reduced benefit is fairly small so it might be worthwhile to go ahead and take the benefit early adding the Spousal Benefit later (more on how this is calculated in later chapters).

Psychological impact. If you simply cannot stand the thought of leaving your Social Security benefit in the government's hands any longer than necessary - and you feel it's to your best interest to start early (even in the face of facts to the contrary) then by all means start early. If that's what it takes to ease your mind you should do it - life's too short to be wrought up over such matters.

On the other hand, maybe Social Security doesn't matter to you. If you have more funds than you really need and the Social Security benefit is of very little real benefit to you - plus if you consider the Social Security system a "safety net" for needy folks, you might want to start much later.

As stated before, in most cases it makes good financial sense for the spouse with the higher earned benefit to delay benefits to age 70, but not in all cases. In order to really get a good handle on how these calculations would work for you it may help to hire a professional advisor to run through the numbers with you.

30. Should I Use IRA Assets or Social Security Benefits?

Folks who have retired or are preparing to retire before the Social Security Full Retirement Age (FRA) face a dilemma if they have IRA assets available. Specifically, is it better to take an income from the IRA account during the years prior to FRA (or as late as age 70) in order to receive a larger Social Security benefit; or should they preserve IRA assets by taking the reduced Social Security benefits at age 62?

At face value, given the nature of IRA assets it seems like the best method would be to preserve the IRA's tax-deferral on those assets even though it means your Social Security benefit will be reduced.

If you look at the taxation of Social Security benefits though, you might discover that delaying receipt of your Social Security benefit will provide a much more tax effective income later in life. In the tables on the next few pages I'll work through the numbers to illustrate what I'm talking about.

Example

For our example, we have an individual who has a pre-tax income requirement of $75,000 per year. The individual has significant IRA assets available. If he takes Social Security at age 62, he will receive $22,500 per year. Delaying Social Security benefits to FRA would get him $30,000; waiting until age 70 would provide a benefit of $39,600 per year. In the tables below and on the next page we show what the tax impact would be for using Social Security at age 62, FRA, and age 70. In each case the required income is always $75,000. We also illustrate the individual living to at least age 90. *(Note: Cost of Living Adjustments (COLAs) are not factored into the examples to provide clarity.)*

Taking Social Security benefit at age 62:

	IRA	SS	Tax
62	$ 52,500	$ 22,500	$ 9,556
63	$ 52,500	$ 22,500	$ 9,556
64	$ 52,500	$ 22,500	$ 9,556
65	$ 52,500	$ 22,500	$ 9,556
66	$ 52,500	$ 22,500	$ 9,556
...			
90	$ 52,500	$ 22,500	$ 9,556
Totals	$ 1,522,500	$ 652,500	$ 277,113

Taking Social Security benefit at age 66:

	IRA	SS	Tax
62	$ 75,000	$ 0	$ 11,113
63	$ 75,000	$ 0	$ 11,113
64	$ 75,000	$ 0	$ 11,113
65	$ 75,000	$ 0	$ 11,113
66	$ 45,000	$ 30,000	$ 7,953
...			
90	$ 45,000	$ 30,000	$ 7,953
Totals	$ 1,425,000	$ 750,000	$ 243,263

Taking Social Security benefit at age 70:			
	IRA	SS	Tax
62	$ 75,000	$ 0	$ 11,113
63	$ 75,000	$ 0	$ 11,113
64	$ 75,000	$ 0	$ 11,113
65	$ 75,000	$ 0	$ 11,113
66	$ 75,000	$ 0	$ 11,113
67	$ 75,000	$ 0	$ 11,113
68	$ 75,000	$ 0	$ 11,113
69	$ 75,000	$ 0	$ 11,113
70	$ 35,400	$ 39,600	$ 5,901
...			
90	$ 35,400	$ 39,600	$ 5,901
Totals	$ 1,343,400	$ 831,600	$ 212,811

The difference you see in the tables is due to the fact that Social Security benefits are at most taxed at an 85% rate. With this in mind, <u>the larger the portion of your required income you can have covered by Social Security, the better.</u> At this income level, the rate is even less, only 85% of the amount above the $44,000 base (the provisional income plus half of the Social Security benefit). This results in almost $34,000 less in taxes paid over the 29-year period illustrated by delaying to age FRA, and nearly $65,000 less in taxes by delaying to age 70.

Note: at higher income levels, this differential will be less significant, but still results in a tax savings by delaying. It should also be noted that COLAs were not factored in, nor was inflation - these factors were eliminated to reduce complexity of the example calculations. In addition, in calculating the tax, deductions and exemptions were not included. At lower income levels, where perhaps the Social Security benefit represents the lion's share of your income, it might make more sense to take the benefit earlier. Each option should be explored in full.

The above example assumes the individual has the available IRA assets to enable delaying receipt of Social Security benefits to a later date. In the end result, delaying to age 70 required less of a total outlay from the IRA, by nearly $180,000, in addition to the tax savings.

Hands down, this is a very significant reason to delay receiving Social Security benefits at least to FRA, and even more reason to delay to age 70. The only factor working against this strategy would be an early, untimely death, especially if the individual in question is not married. In that case the IRA assets would have been used up much more quickly than necessary, and no surviving spouse is available to carry on with the Social Security survivor benefit.

31. The Do-Over

The decision of when to begin taking your Social Security retirement benefit is very important. The problem is, otftentimes we are not in a position to delay receiving the benefit. Or maybe we didn't consider what a difference it would make to delay taking payment (it's substantial).

It's a little-known fact that you can re-set your Social Security payout amount during the first twelve months after initiating the benefit. You may have heard of this, but usually discussions have few details on how to do it. Plus, the rules changed recently (in 2010), so you might need a refresher.

Let's say for example you had a choice to begin your Social Security payout at 62 at a reduced amount of $750 per month or waiting until "normal" retirement age (66) when your benefit could be 33% greater, at $1,000 per month. (For the purposes of simplicity of illustration, the annual cost-of-living increases have not been included in this example.)

Yes, these are real world numbers, and yes, the difference is that great. However, if you change your mind within the <u>first 12 months</u> of receiving your benefit you have the option of paying back all of the benefits you've received to-date and waiting to apply later – with no consequence. The money you received for the first (up to) 12 months could be a no-interest loan, if you wanted to work it that way. Of course the consequences of not getting this right could be very costly.

So how does it work? It's fairly simple - you pay back the Social Security Administration all of the money which has been paid out since you initiated the benefit. That's it, no interest, no penalties. Then you can re-apply for benefits at your current age or later if you wish.

The only problem with the whole plan is this: you can only do this once and it's not revocable. So if you sent in your payback to the SSA yesterday and accidentally stepped in front of a bus today, your heirs do not get the money back. However, as is the case with each of these decisions, if you are the higher wage earner and your spouse survives you, he or she would be eligible to receive the increased amount (to your age of death) as a Survivor Benefit.

Obviously this isn't a consideration for everyone and it may not be an appropriate decision for many who do have the funds available to make such a move, but for some folks in specific situations it can be a pretty good move. As mentioned numerous times in this book, as long as you are in good health, the longer you wait to start taking the Social Security benefit the better. This is especially true for the higher earning spouse.

32. History of the Do-Over

On December 8, 2010 the Social Security Administration published a revision to their "withdrawal policy".

What Changed?

Essentially SSA decided the original rule represented a little too good of a deal, even though very few people ever took advantage of it. The original rule in brief, allowed an individual to begin taking retirement benefits at any age above 62 and then at *any point* in the future the individual could pay back *all of the benefits* (without interest) and re-set his or her beginning date for receiving benefits. This strategy allowed the individual to receive benefits and invest them, then pay back the entire amount (but keep any interest earned or growth) and then receive a higher benefit due to the credits for delaying retirement.

Under the new rules you can still use this strategy but the payback is only allowed <u>within the first 12 months</u> of your receiving benefits. This doesn't mean you have to re-set your benefit immediately and continue receiving benefits - you could pay back your benefit at 12 months or less and withdraw from receiving benefits until much later if you wish.

So the key here is you couldn't for example begin receiving benefits at age 62, then at age 70 pay it all back and re-set. Those were the days, my friend. We thought they'd never end. But they did.

Under the revised rule, you're limited to only 12 months of received benefits before you pay it back. For example, you could receive benefits at age 62 until you've received 12 months' worth, then stop receiving benefits and pay back what you received. After you've paid back the benefits you could delay reinstating your benefit until FRA or age 70 or whenever you like. Or, at age 63 you could pay it back and re-set to a benefit for your new attained age.

33. Spousal Benefits in Cases of Divorce

We covered the Spousal Benefit for Social Security retirement benefits earlier. It is also important to note that similar benefits are available to divorced spouses.

A divorced spouse is eligible for a Social Security Spousal Benefit based upon the PIA (Primary Insurance Amount) of his or her ex-spouse under the following conditions:

- he or she is at least 62 years of age;

- the couple was married for ten years or longer;

- he or she is not currently married; and

- he or she is not receiving a benefit (on his or her own record or another ex-spouse's record) that is greater than the benefit based on this particular ex-spouse's record.

The former spouse does not have to have applied for benefits, as long as the couple have been divorced for at least two years* when he or she applies for the Spousal Benefit. However, the former spouse must be <u>eligible</u> for benefits - that is, he or she (the former spouse) must be at least age 62. The Spousal Benefit for the divorced individual is always based upon the Primary Insurance Amount (PIA) of the ex-spouse, and the regular reduction rules apply as if the two were still married (see Chapter 7).

As with the Spousal Benefit for currently married couples, if the divorcee reaches FRA and is eligible for a benefit on his or her own record, the divorcee can choose to receive only the divorced Spousal Benefit now and delay receiving retirement benefits in order to build delay credits, increasing the benefit available on his or her own account.

Any benefits received by the divorcee have no impact on benefits to be received by the former spouse, any other ex-spouses of the former spouse or the former spouse's current spouse and dependents. The ex-spouse receiving benefits also does not impact the Family Maximum Benefit (see Chapter 9 for more on the Family Maximum Benefit calculation).

There's a set of circumstances that opens up a unique option for divorced folks which is not available to married folks: both members of the ex-couple can file a Restricted Application for Spousal Benefits at the same time.

If a couple is married, in order to file a Restricted Application for Spousal Benefits, the other spouse must have already filed for his or her own benefits. However, if a divorced couple has not remarried, they are each at Full Retirement Age, and the divorce has been finalized for at least two years, the requirement for the other spouse to have filed does not apply – which makes both spouses eligible to file a Restricted Application. See Chapter 36 for more on the Restricted Application.

* In the event that the ex-spouse has filed for his or her own benefit, the two-year delay does not apply. If Sam and Dana (both age 62) are divorced after a 10-year marriage in order for Dana to receive Spousal Benefits based on Sam's record one of two things must happen: either Sam must have filed for his own Social Security retirement benefit or Dana must wait until two years after the divorce has been finalized.

34. Remarriage and Spousal Benefits

The Social Security Administration treats former spouses differently from widows and widowers with regard to benefits when the person in question remarries. This only affects ex-spouses when the other partner from the former marriage is still living. When the former spouse dies the surviving spouse is treated as a widow or widower.

Remarriage Rules for Widows and Widowers

(For brevity I'm going to refer only to widows, but everything here applies to widowers as well.)

If a widow is under age 60 and remarries (and stays married) she is no longer eligible for a Survivor Benefit based upon her late husband's record. After age 60 the widow can remarry and retain access to Survivor Benefits on her late spouse's record. This rule applies the same way for a widow who was divorced from the decedent as long as she was married to the ex-spouse for at least 10 years.

Remarriage Rules for Ex-Spouses

If a couple was married for at least 10 years and has been divorced for at least 2 years, the ex-spouse can be eligible for Spousal Benefits based upon his or her former spouse's record - as long as he or she remains unmarried. Her or his ex-spouse must be eligible for benefits (doesn't have to be taking them) and she or he must be at least age 62 for early benefits. The same rules apply as if they were still married except the ex-spouse doesn't have to apply for benefits to enable her or him to be eligible for the Spousal Benefit.

However - if she or he marries at any time while the ex is still alive she or he will be ineligible for the spousal benefit while married. If there is a subsequent divorce or the current spouse dies the divorcee's eligibility is restored. When the first ex-spouse (or any applicable earlier ex-spouse) dies, the divorcee becomes eligible for a Survivor's Benefit as a Widow(er) (see above for remarriage rules for Widows). The divorcee can choose any ex-spouse (if he or she was married more than once) with the highest available benefit for his or her Spousal and/or Survivor Benefit - as long as she or he met the eligibility (length of marriage) to the former spouse.

35. Delayed Benefits

It's usually best, for most things in the financial world, to act now rather than waiting 'til later. The notable exception is with regard to applying for Social Security benefits.

As you'll see from the table below, if you're in the group born after 1943 (that's you, Boomers!) you can increase the amount of your Social Security benefit by 8% for every year you delay receiving benefits after your Full Retirement Age (FRA).

Delaying Receipt of Benefits to Increase the Amount

If you are delaying your retirement beyond FRA, you'll increase the amount of benefit you are eligible to receive. Depending upon your year of birth, this amount will be 8% per year (these days) you delay receiving benefits - which can tally up to an increase of as much as 32%. See the table on the next page for the increase amounts per year based upon birth year:

Maximum Delay Credit Adjustments

Birth Year	FRA	Delay Credit	Maximum (age 70)
1940	65 & 6 mos.	7%	131½%
1941	65 & 8 mos.	7½%	132½%
1942	65 & 10 mos.	7½%	131¼%
1943-1954	66	8%	132%
1955	66 & 2 mos.	8%	130⅔%
1956	66 & 4 mos.	8%	129⅓%
1957	66 & 6 mos.	8%	128%
1958	66 & 8 mos.	8%	126⅔%
1959	66 & 10 mos.	8%	125⅓%
1960 & later	67	8%	124%

Source: Social Security Administration

As displayed above, you can receive as much as a 57% higher benefit payment by delaying to age 70 versus starting benefits at age 62. (*Note: the 57% higher benefit is based on receiving a 75% benefit when filing early, versus an increased 132% benefit when filing later.*) The decision between filing early and filing later should also account for the additional years you will be receiving the benefit if you file early, because in the earlier years your total received benefit will be more than if you file later. This advantage to filing early tends to go away as the break-even point is reached by your early 80's.

An Example

Here's an example of the benefit of delay in action:

You were born in 1949, and as such your FRA is age 66. According to the benefit statement you've received from Social Security, you are eligible for a monthly benefit payment of $2,000 when you reach your FRA (which would be in 2015). If you delayed applying for your benefit until the next year, your monthly benefit payment would be $2,160 per month - an increase of $1,920 per year. If you delayed until age 68 (two years after FRA), the monthly payment would be increased to $2,320, for an annual increase of $3,840. At age 69, delaying would increase your annual benefit by $5,760, and at age 70, your monthly payment would be $2,640, for an annual benefit of $31,680 - $7,680 more than at FRA. This amounts to a 32% increase in your benefit by delaying receipt of the benefit by 4 years!

Notes

It's important to note that this is not a compounding increase - that is, your increased benefit from one year is not multiplied by the increase for the following year. The factor for each year (or portion of a year) is simply added to the factor(s) from prior years. You also don't have to wait a full year to achieve some delayed retirement benefit - this delay is calculated on a monthly basis, so if you delayed by 6 months your increase would be 4% over the FRA amount.

By delaying benefits you will not only possibly increase the amount you will receive over your lifetime, but also the Survivor Benefit your spouse will receive upon your passing. For some folks this can make a huge difference as they plan for the inevitable.

36. A Twist on Spousal Benefits

In this chapter we discuss an option available to all married recipients of Social Security retirement benefits - but you might not have thought of it. For most married couples, it makes a good deal of sense for the spouse with the higher wage base - that is, the spouse who has earned the most money throughout his or her working career - to delay receiving Social Security retirement benefits as long as possible.

As described in Chapter 35 about credits for delaying Social Security benefits, each year you delay receiving your Social Security retirement benefit past your full retirement age (FRA) can result in an 8% increase in your benefit amount. When delaying like this, it often also makes sense for the spouse with the lower wage base to begin receiving benefits at the lower rate, either at the early retirement age of 62, or upon reaching FRA. Then later, when the spouse with the higher wage base begins taking the increased, delayed benefits, the spouse with the lower wage base will be eligible to receive the Spousal Benefit, based upon one-half of the higher wage base spouse's benefit.

But Wait, There's More!

What most folks don't realize is that while the spouse with the lower wage base is receiving the reduced benefit, the spouse with the higher wage base can apply for a Spousal Benefit based upon one-half of the lower wage base spouse's benefit, beginning at the higher wage base spouse's reaching FRA.

While this doesn't necessarily amount to a very large payment, it is money you are entitled to and should receive. The spouse with the higher wage base can receive this Spousal Benefit from FRA up to the time when election is made to begin receiving the delayed benefit based on his or her own record, at age 70. Then the spouse with the lower wage base can begin receiving the Spousal Benefit based upon the higher wage base spouse's benefit as well.

Quick Example

Let's say Jane and Bob are a typical couple - Jane didn't work outside the home while their children were in school, while Bob has worked and earned Social Security credits since age 21. As a result Jane's PIA is considerably lower than Bob's. (Keep in mind, the roles could easily be reversed.)

So at age 62, Jane begins drawing her Social Security retirement benefit, in the amount of $750 per month (Jane's PIA is $1,000). They have decided to delay Bob's benefit as long as possible, to his age 70. Once Bob reaches FRA when both of them are age 66, he can now begin drawing a restricted spousal benefit based upon Jane's PIA. So Bob can draw a Spousal Benefit equal to 50% of Jane's PIA, or $500 per month.

When the couple reaches age 70 Bob applies for and begins receiving his full delayed benefit - which is approximately $3,300 per month (PIA of $2,500). Jane's Spousal Benefit will be based upon the difference between her PIA and 50% of Bob's PIA - $1,250 minus $1,000 equals $250. This is added to her own benefit for a total of $1,000.

That's all there is to it. It may not seem like a lot of money, but why would you not go for it? The key here is that the Spousal Benefit Bob can receive at this stage ($500) is greater than the spousal offset Jane can receive ($250) since she's collecting her retirement benefit at the same time. So it makes fiscal sense for Bob to continue delaying receipt of benefits and apply for the Spousal Benefit at FRA. As we noted in our discussion earlier about Survivor's Benefits – there is no impact on Jane's Survivor Benefit (from Bob's record) since she has filed early.

When Bob makes the request for this special type of Spousal Benefit, specific language is necessary. When discussing this with the Social Security Administration, Bob needs to specifically state that he wishes to submit a "Restricted Application for Spousal Benefits only". This way the SSA folks will (eventually) get the point – otherwise he will likely hear many incorrect responses to his request, such as he can't do this. The common response from SSA when requesting a Spousal Benefit in this fashion is that your own benefit is greater than half of the PIA of your spouse, so it's not allowed. That's incorrect if you are submitting a "restricted application for Spousal Benefits only".

It's important to note this strategy and the typical File and Suspend strategy cannot be used at the same time by the same person (refer back to the Primer in Chapter 0 for this rule). One spouse could File and Suspend and the other file a Restricted Application though. We'll talk about File and Suspend next.

37. File and Suspend

This is another provision of the Social Security system which should be filed under the "Little Known Facts" section - although it is becoming more known these days. How it works and what's important about it is the subject of this chapter.

How File and Suspend Works and Why It's Important

Any worker can establish a benefit amount by applying at any time. But - after Full Retirement Age he or she doesn't have to continue receiving the benefit. The worker can immediately suspend the receipt of benefits, so seemingly the application is unnecessary. However, what this has done is establish a "base" for the worker's spouse (and other dependents) to begin receiving benefits based upon the worker's record.

Here's an example:

Hiram is at Full Retirement Age (FRA) and his wife Lois is the same age. Lois has a much lower benefit available based on her own record. She is looking forward to utilizing Hiram's earnings record to receive the Spousal Benefit.

At the same time, the couple prefers to delay receiving Hiram's benefit as long as possible, to age 70, in order to receive the maximum increases. To achieve both goals Hiram applies for benefits at FRA and then immediately suspends receiving the benefit. This establishes the amount Lois can begin receiving in Spousal Benefits while at the same time allowing Hiram's record to continue increasing in value until he reaches age 70, the maximum age to delay.

How To Do It

Although the mechanics of this option became available in 2000, the Social Security Administration (SSA) personnel are sometimes *still* not familiar with it. Because of this it is probably in your best interest to visit your local SSA office in person to complete the process. This way you can work with the staff (and perhaps managers) face-to-face to make sure you apply as you intend to.

In order to ensure the SSA personnel are clear about what you're doing, you should download the Social Security Legislative Bulletin 106-20 (the link is at the end of this chapter) which explains the provision fully. The provision is part of the Senior Citizens' Freedom to Work Act of 2000 - and the third bullet point of the Bulletin is what you want to point out as proof that you can pull this number.

Soon enough SSA personnel are going to get this one straight as more and more folks do this maneuver, so be patient with them. Print out the bulletin and take it with you to make sure you get what you're asking for. The bulletin can also be found in Appendix A and you can find a printable copy of the bulletin at the following web address:

www.SocialSecurityOwnersManual.com/bulletin-106-20/

38. Deemed Filing

Earlier I mentioned how deemed filing impacts a person younger than FRA who is eligible for Spousal Benefits at the same time as he or she first files for retirement benefits. In a case like this, deemed filing rules require that the Spousal Benefit is applied for at the same time as the retirement benefit for the individual.

There are a couple of circumstances which have to be in place for deemed filing to take effect. First of all, the spouse in question must be at least 62 years of age, but less than Full Retirement Age. Secondly, the other spouse must have filed for his or her retirement benefit – either before or at the same time. The second spouse could have suspended receiving benefits after filing; the key is he or she has filed making the first spouse eligible for Spousal Benefits.

Often this deemed filing provision doesn't matter to a couple – if one spouse is filing for benefits early, adding the reduced Spousal Benefit is just extra gravy on top. However, it might be advantageous for the couple's overall financial picture to delay receiving the Spousal Benefit until FRA. It's possible to coordinate this but you have to play your cards right.

The second requirement for deemed filing to take effect is that the second spouse has filed for benefits. If this spouse has not filed for benefits on his or her own record at the point when the first spouse files, then deemed filing does not apply.

What this means is if you can plan when each spouse is filing for benefits, you can effectively avoid the impact of deemed filing.

Here's an example: Fred and Ethel, ages 65 and 61 respectively, hope to maximize their Social Security benefits. Fred, with a January birthdate, has earned the maximum wages over his lifetime and Ethel, with a February birthdate, has earned a much smaller benefit during her lifetime. To maximize their Social Security benefits over their lifetimes the plan is for Ethel to file for her own benefit as soon as she reaches age 62. Fred is going to delay his benefits to age 70 for the maximum benefit, both in his lifetime and in Ethel's lifetime if she survives him.

Complicating matters, Fred and Ethel are the legal guardians of their two grandsons, Chip and Ernie, ages 8 and 10. It is their desire to provide Chip and Ernie with dependent's benefits based upon Fred's earnings record.

The dependent's benefits could be provided based upon Fred's record now if he were to file for his retirement benefit, but that would thwart the plan to maximize Fred's benefits by delaying to age 70. On the other hand, at some point at or after Fred's Full Retirement Age he could file and suspend, thereby providing Chip and Ernie with the filed record in order to begin receiving dependent's benefits.

The problem is if Fred files and suspends immediately upon reaching FRA (in January), he will make Ethel eligible for Spousal Benefits when she plans to file for her own retirement benefit in February when she turns 62.

Let's tally this up: Fred wants to provide the dependent's benefits for Chip and Ernie based on his own record. At the same time Ethel would like to receive her retirement benefit only (and not the Spousal Benefit) until she reaches FRA.

The way to accomplish this would be for Fred to delay his file and suspend action until at least one month after Ethel files for her retirement benefit. This way when Ethel files she would not be eligible for the Spousal Benefit (because Fred has not filed), and so deemed filing will not require her to take the Spousal Benefit. Then, at least a month later Fred will file for his own retirement benefit and immediately suspend. This way the filing record has been established so Chip and Ernie can begin receiving their dependent's benefits based on Fred's record.

If Fred filed at any time before Ethel's filing (or in the same month), then deemed filing would take effect and she could no longer delay the receipt of her Spousal Benefit. Using the timing strategy detailed above will ensure their plans can go as they expected.

39. Coordinating Spousal Benefits

You know from the preceding chapters there are quite a few components to keep in mind as you and your spouse plan for your Social Security retirement benefits. It can be a challenge to work through all of them on your own. To help you with this process, below is a guideline which you might find helpful as you plan. The point of this rule of thumb is to attain the highest benefit for the longest surviving spouse while maximizing total lifetime benefits for both spouses.

The Spousal Coordination Rule of Thumb

First of all, we have to make some assumptions:

- in this case, we assume the spouses are the same age (within a year);

- we're using the rate of inflation as the rate to discount future money to present value;

- we assume any money received in Social Security benefits is offset by not taking the same amount from your savings (in order for the rule to work, your savings must earn at least 1% more than the rate of inflation); and lastly,

- we are not making a "guesstimate" of the date of death for either spouse.

Scenario 1: if the lower Primary Insurance Amount (PIA) is greater than 1/3 of the higher PIA, then the lower earner should take benefits on his or her own record at age 62. Then the higher earner takes advantage of the Spousal Benefit upon reaching Full Retirement Age (FRA) by filing a restricted application. Finally, the higher earner takes his or her own benefit at age 70, maximizing his or her lifetime benefit (and his or her spouse's Survivor Benefit). If allowable, that is to say, if the amount of the lower earner's PIA is less than 50% of the higher earner's PIA upon filing for benefits at age 70, the lower earner should also take the Spousal Benefit at that time.

Scenario 2: if the lower PIA is less than 1/3 of the higher PIA, once again the lower earner begins taking his or her own benefit at age 62, as soon as eligible. The higher earner files and suspends at FRA providing a base for the lower earner to begin taking the Spousal Benefit. And finally, the higher earner takes his or her own benefit at age 70, again maximizing the lifetime and Survivor's benefits.

I won't go into the details of all the specific calculations required for these two tactics to work their magic - because as with all rules of thumb there are bound to be specific differences in your own situation which will impact the outcome. Use these rules as a guide to help you think about the options, but put a pencil to the actual figures for your situation and make sure they make sense for you.

40. Spousal Coordination Scenarios

There still may be some confusion about the best way to coordinate these benefits to the maximum potential. This chapter will follow a typical couple through the process using several scenarios so you can see the potential outcomes of various options.

Our Example Couple

Our couple for the purpose of these examples is named Lester and Selma, both age 60. The couple's future potential monthly benefits are reported as follows:

Spousal Coordination Survivor Benefit Example

Age	Lester	Selma
62	$1,852	$1,222
66	$2,469	$1,629
70	$3,259	$2,150

Note: These figures merely give us an example to work with. We've purposely set the couple to equal ages in order to simplify the calculations.

First Option: Both File Early (age 62)

Lester and Selma are bothered by the fact they've had FICA (Federal Income Contributions Act, otherwise known as Social Security) withholding from their paychecks over their entire working lives, so they have decided that as soon as possible they're going to start taking their hard-earned Social Security benefit. Let's look at the resulting amounts this couple will receive over their lifetimes, assuming they both live to age 95:

Age	Lester	Selma	Total
95	$755,616	$498,576	$1,254,192

Seems like a pretty decent result, don't you think? But as we know, things don't always go the way we expect. Let's see what the outcome is if Lester were to die at age 72:

Age	Lester	Selma	Total
72	$244,464	$161,304	
95		$723,516	$967,980

The increased accumulated amount Selma received over her lifetime is because she began receiving Lester's benefit as a Survivor's Benefit upon his death. Actually, Selma receives a bit of an increase, up to 82.5% of Lester's benefit, due to a little-known fact about Survivor Benefit minimums (see Chapter 8 for more on the Survivor Benefit).

Now let's shake this up a bit and see what other outcomes we can see.

Option 2: Both File at FRA (age 66)

Having thought things over, Lester and Selma change their minds and decide to delay receiving their benefit until age 66, Full Retirement Age for each of them. Here's what happens if they both live to age 95:

	Start Age 66			Start Age 62		
Age	Lester	Selma	Total	Lester	Selma	Total
95	$888,840	$586,440	$1,475,280	$755,616	$498,576	$1,254,192

And again, since the likelihood of Selma's outliving Lester is significant, we look at the outcome if Lester passes away at age 72:

	Start Age 66			Start Age 62		
Age	Lester	Selma	Total	Lester	Selma	Total
72	$207,396	$136,836		$244,464	$161,304	
95		$818,280	$1,025,676		$723,516	$967,980

This is where it starts to get interesting. If you'll notice, under this option when they both live to age 95 they are receiving a significant amount more by taking the Full Retirement Age amounts - a total of $1,475,280 versus $1,254,192 when filing early. This is an increase of $221,088.

Delaying start of benefits is also more advantageous when Lester predeceases Selma. When taking the early payment option Selma would receive a total of $723,516 over her lifetime, while if they both delay receiving benefits to age 66, she'll receive $818,280, or $94,764 more in lifetime benefits. When you add in Lester's benefit over his lifetime to age 72, the Full Retirement Age option pays out $1,025,676 combined, versus $967,980 under the early option. This is a difference of $57,696 more in total lifetime benefits for the couple.

So we have a rule of thumb which fits this couple's circumstances: <u>It pays off in the long run to delay receiving benefits to a later age.</u>

Option 3: Both File at Maximum (Age 70)

Here are the results when both delay filing for retirement benefits to the maximum age of 70:

Age	Start Age 70			Start Age 66		
	Lester	Selma	Total	Lester	Selma	Total
95	$1,016,808	$670,800	$1,687,608	$888,840	$586,440	$1,475,280

And here's the outcome if Lester dies at age 72:

Age	Start Age 70			Start Age 66		
	Lester	Selma	Total	Lester	Selma	Total
72	$117,324	$136,632		$207,396	$136,836	
95		1,036,116	$1,153,440		$818,280	$1,025,676

As you probably expected, the total for both life outcomes is better yet with the option of waiting to age 70 to file. If both Lester and Selma live to age 95 they'll collect a total of $1,687,608 in benefits. The benefit is also greater if Lester dies at age 72, as illustrated above.

Our rule of thumb from above still holds true. But we've not necessarily learned anything else, beyond the fact that the rule of thumb becomes more significant the more you delay - up to age 70 (no advantage to delaying beyond age 70).

So, that's it, right? It's best to wait until age 70 to begin taking your Social Security retirement benefits - cut and dried. Hold on there, pardner! Let's have another look at the numbers and the provisions of the system.

Option 4: Selma files early (age 62), Lester files at maximum (age 70)

Here are the outcomes:

Age	Lester @70	Selma @62	Total	Lester @70	Selma @70	Total
95	$1,016,808	$498,576	$1,515,384	$1,016,808	$670,800	$1,687,608

And if Lester dies at age 72:

Age	Lester @70	Selma @62	Total	Lester @70	Selma @70	Total
72	$117,324	$161,304		$117,324	$136,632	
95		$1,060,788	$1,178,112		$1,036,116	$1,153,440

This one takes a little bit longer to digest what happened. If you look at the totals, you'll quickly see that when Selma files at age 62 and both live to age 95, it's still better in the long run to delay receiving benefits for Selma. (For brevity, we've only included Option 3 to compare with, since it had the best outcome of the first three.)

But when you look at the possibility of Lester's dying at age 72, something different happens: the couple's lifetime benefits are greater if Selma starts taking her benefit early and Lester delays to age 70. This is because Selma is receiving her benefit for 8 years (even though it's significantly reduced) earlier than the Option 3 choice - and then when Lester dies she begins taking her Survivor Benefit option at Lester's maximum amount. When you calculate the lifetime benefit received, Selma and Lester would receive more - $24,672 in total - when Selma files at age 62, Lester at the maximum age of 70, if Lester dies at age 72.

This illustrates how Option 4 works out to a better conclusion if the higher wage earner dies early. This doesn't tell us a lot, and it doesn't conclusively give us another rule of thumb, so let's make another change.

Option 5: Same as Option 4, but Lester dies at age 80

So, is the outcome we found in Option 4 only good if Lester dies relatively early? What happens if he lives a while longer, say to age 80? Here's what happens:

Age	Lester @70	Selma @62	Total	Lester @70	Selma @70	Total
80	$430,188	$278,616		$430,188	$343,032	
95		$865,236	$1,295,424		$929,652	$1,359,840

Just before age 80 is the break-even point between these two strategies. If Lester (at these benefit levels) lives to this age or later, then the strategy of delaying both benefits to age 70 works out best.

So, for this couple, if Lester (with the higher benefit) dies relatively soon after starting benefits it makes sense for Selma (the lower-benefit spouse) to file early. The same would be true if Selma predeceases Lester.

How does this help? You aren't likely to know one another's expected longevity, and you really shouldn't plan to bump off your spouse just to make the numbers work out for you. You can take cues from your family history, present health, and the like, but in the end you just have to make a judgment call.

Some Final Notes

Bear in mind the examples above are specific to this couple's circumstances only. Your mileage may vary – in fact your mileage <u>will</u> vary, unless you happen to have those exact same earnings levels (now that would be a coincidence!).

To keep from confusing matters too much, in our examples we did not factor in Cost-of-Living-Adjustments - to keep things as simple to understand as possible.

There can be other alternatives to look at which are significant - especially if there is a substantial difference in the ages of the two spouses. We'll look at some of these situations in the next chapter.

41. More Spousal Coordination Scenarios

As mentioned in the previous chapter, when there is a substantial difference in the ages of spouses there can be some differences to consider when coordinating Social Security benefits. Let's work through some examples with variances in the couples' ages.

Logan and Hyacinth

Logan is 62 and Hyacinth is 58. Logan has a PIA of $800 and Hyacinth's is $2,000. Right off, you might notice that it is probably going to be in this couple's best interest to delay Hyacinth's filing as late as possible in order to maximize their overall benefits. Let's review the outcomes for a few scenarios for this couple.

If both Logan and Hyacinth file for all available benefits as early as possible, then Logan will file for his own benefit at 62, Hyacinth will file for her own benefit at 62, and then Logan will be eligible to file for the Spousal Benefit at age 66 (since Hyacinth has filed for her benefit at this time). Here is the outcome for the couple if they both live to age 95:

Scenario 1

Age	Logan	Hyacinth	Total
95	$316,800	$605,064	$921,864

And here is the way the benefits work out if Logan were to pass away at age 72, which is the more likely outcome since men have a shorter expected lifespan and Logan is older to begin with:

Scenario 1, Logan dies @72

Age	Logan	Hyacinth	Total
72	$96,000	$124,572	
95		$605,064	$701,064

Hyacinth's lifetime benefit will not increase in this example since her own benefit is greater than a Survivor Benefit based upon Logan's record. So what happens if Hyacinth pre-deceases Logan at her age 72?

Scenario 1, Hyacinth dies @72

Age	Logan	Hyacinth	Total
72	$134,400	$195,756	
95	$510,600		$706,356

Next we'll look at what would happen if Hyacinth delays her benefit to Full Retirement Age (for her it would be 66 years and 4 months), and Logan files at 62, waiting to file for the Spousal Benefit until he is 70 years and 4 months old when Hyacinth has filed.

Scenario 2 v. Scenario 1

Age	Logan @62	Hyacinth @66.33	Total	Logan @62	Hyacinth @62	Total
95	$307,200	$724,680	$1,031,880	$316,800	$605,064	$921,864

As you can see, there is an increase in the couple's overall benefit of approximately $110,000 by delaying Hyacinth's benefit to her Full Retirement Age. To continue with our example, we'll see what the outcome would be if Logan dies at age 72:

Scenario 2 v. Scenario 1, Logan dies @72

Age	Logan @62	Hyacinth @66.33	Total	Logan @62	Hyacinth @62	Total
72	$86,400	$169,092		$96,000	$124,572	
95		$724,680	$811,080		$605,064	$701,064

The increase here is approximately the same as before, which is to be expected since Hyacinth's benefit is the only change, other than the fact that Logan must delay filing for the Spousal Benefit until he reaches 70 years and 4 months of age, the same time that Hyacinth reaches FRA.

What if Hyacinth were to die before Logan? Below is the outcome if Hyacinth passed away at her age 72:

Scenario 2 v. Scenario 1, Hyacinth dies @72

Age	Logan @62	Hyacinth @66.33	Total	Logan @62	Hyacinth @62	Total
72	$124,800	$169,092		$134,400	$195,756	
95	$583,764		$752,856	$510,600		$706,356

The differential is less in this example, but still an increase when Hyacinth delays her benefit to FRA. As you know, since Logan's benefit is so much less than Hyacinth's benefit, upon her death Logan will be entitled to a Survivor Benefit equal to Hyacinth's former benefit.

Let's see what the differences are when Hyacinth delays her benefit to age 70 while also filing and suspending at FRA:

Scenario 3 v. Scenario 2

Age	Logan @62	Hyacinth @70	Total	Logan @62	Hyacinth @66.33	Total
95	$307,200	$815,256	$1,122,456	$307,200	$724,680	$1,031,880

Here we see an increase of more than $90,000 over the option when Hyacinth files at FRA. This is due to the fact that she's receiving her delay-increased benefit over her lifetime.

We determined earlier that if Logan dies relatively young the change to the outcome is insignificant, so we won't review that outcome again. What happens if Hyacinth passes away at the age of 72?

Scenario 3 v. Scenario 2, Hyacinth dies @72

Age	Logan @62	Hyacinth @70	Total	Logan @62	Hyacinth @66.33	Total
72	$124,800	$94,068		$86,400	$169,092	
95	$720,564		$814,632	$583,764		$752,856

Here, since Hyacinth's benefit is so much greater from the delay credits, when she passes away Logan will be eligible for the increased benefit that Hyacinth has been receiving, which results in a lifetime benefit increase of more than $60,000.

Let's review one more adjustment for this couple: Logan delays his filing to age 70 and Hyacinth also delays her receipt of benefits to age 70. She will file and suspend at FRA of 66 years and 4 months, which allows Logan to file for Spousal Benefits at the age of 70 years and 4 months. Here is the outcome:

Scenario 4 v. Scenario 3

Age	Logan @70	Hyacinth @70	Total	Logan @62	Hyacinth @70	Total
95	$329,472	$815,256	$1,144,728	$307,200	$815,256	$1,122,456

Not a significant differential here since Logan's dollar-benefit increase is relatively small when he's receiving the maximum delay credits.

So, for this couple, the most significant strategic option in terms of total dollar benefits is to delay Hyacinth's benefit to her age 70. The timing of Logan's filing does not make much of an impact, so filing earlier is likely the best option in order to maximize the number of years he is receiving this benefit.

Part 5: The Future of Social Security

42. Solvency

For most folks, the Social Security system and how it works is a mystery. Many believe there is an account somewhere with your name on it, and you'll get to draw funds from the account when you retire. Other folks will tell you the system is bankrupt or nearly so. Still others will swear it's a Ponzi scheme.

These are mostly myths. So what is the truth?

How The Social Security System Works

In a way, the Social Security system actually *does* resemble a Ponzi scheme, since the early participants paid in very little and received an inordinately large benefit (by comparison to what they paid in) – while later participants will be paying in a far larger amount, possibly more than they will ever get back out in benefits. To be a true Ponzi scheme though the later participants would be told they can expect the same return on investment that the earlier folks received. I think we've understood for quite some time that this isn't an investment but a tax – and ultimately we may get very little out of the system compared to what we put into it.

Another, possibly more accurate way to look at Social Security is that it is a longevity insurance policy and the policy's terms for payout are becoming much more restrictive. It is possible that, as with many insurance policies, you will pay the premiums and never get to file a claim, or the claim that you file will have a much lower payout than you expected.

From the beginning the Social Security system has overtly been a "pay as you go" system, meaning current receipts from tax withholding are used to pay benefits to current recipients. Most of the time during its 80-year existence the system has been paying out less in benefits than it was taking in from withholding, and so the surplus has been placed in a trust fund[2] to help pay for benefits in the future. This trust fund amounts to roughly $2.7 trillion these days.

This design was based on the incorrect assumption that each succeeding generation would be larger than the previous generation, therefore the receipts would always be greater than the payouts. That was before the Baby Boom.

Since 2010 the Social Security payouts have been greater than the non-interest income (primarily tax rolls), and the interest generated by the trust fund's account will be enough to cover the excess needs of

---

[2] Much has been said and written about the "trust fund". It should be understood there is no such account with the $2.7 trillion in the balance. Congress has long since raided the trust fund and presently has a huge I.O.U. in the account. It's not clear how this I.O.U. will ever be paid off – stay tuned for more as we get to the days when trust fund monies will be needed to pay current benefits.

the system through 2020. At that point it is projected the principal in the trust fund will be accessed to pay benefits, and the trust fund principal is expected to be exhausted by 2033. From 2033 onward unless something changes, only 77% of promised benefits can be paid.

So – What's Going to Happen?

I can't tell the future, but I have a couple of guesses as to what may occur. But first, I wanted to point out a couple of recent developments:

1) In 2010, due in part to the economic downturn, the Social Security system paid out more than it took in. This trend has continued through 2013, to most recent trustee report as of this printing. Stay tuned, but also see #2.

2) The long-term trend which will likely have the greatest impact on the health of the Social Security system is the delay of retirement among many Americans, specifically the trendsetting Baby Boom generation. According to recent data, the percentage of folks between 65 and 75 who are still active in the workforce was 25% in 2010, versus 17% in 1990. That's a significant fact because those folks are continuing to pay into the system and either delaying receipt of benefits or receiving a smaller benefit (at least until Full Retirement Age) than was projected.

The impact of this combination of factors is unknown but the overall outlook for the system has not improved over the past several years, and nothing has been done to systematically resolve the situation.

My Guesses

In the meantime, here are my guesses as to what may happen:

- Like anyone with a finite budget, when it comes time to begin paying out of principal there will need to be cut-backs. I expect for benefits to be reduced across the board – possibly by as much as 25%.

- But before that happens, I expect we'll see increases to the ages for benefits, such as bumping up the early retirement age from 62 to 64, and the maximum benefit age from 70 to 72. These increases would match the increase to the Full Retirement Age which has been in place for some time now.

- Expect some sort of means testing to begin – meaning if you have other sources of income (IRA, pension, 401(k), etc.) then your Social Security benefit will likely be reduced and possibly eliminated.

- Expect to see the tax ceiling (the maximum earnings taxed by Social Security tax) to be increased. This one seems like a no brainer, but it seems to get very little traction when recommended as a revenue enhancer.

- And lastly, plan for pretty much any benefit you receive to be taxed to some degree.

Regardless, all this talk about Social Security going bankrupt is ill-founded. Since the system has the ability to draw in tax rolls it cannot be bankrupted; benefits can decrease and ages for benefits can increase, but it can't go completely broke. It's bad, but not catastrophic.

For an interesting exercise, my friend and colleague Tom Nowak recommends checking out the website http://www.actuary.org/socialsecurity/game.html (or search "AARP Social Security Tool") where you can see for yourself how easy it could be to fix Social Security by making a few minor adjustments in the manner that was done in the 80's.

So What Can You Do?

Write your congressmen & women. Light a candle. Wring your hands, and say "oh my". And in the end you may just have to learn to get over it and realize Social Security may not be counted upon as a significant portion of your retirement income – especially if you were born after about 1955. Concentrate on bolstering your savings, and then if the Social Security fairy happens to leave something on your potatoes when you retire, consider it gravy.

43. Methods of Calculation of COLAs

One of the many proposed changes which is being considered to help resolve the current budgetary issues is to change the index used to adjust Social Security benefits from the current method, using the Consumer Price Index for Urban Wage Earners and Clerical Workers, or CPI-W, to a much more conservative index known as the Chained Consumer Price Index for all Urban Consumers (or C-CPI-U). (See Chapter 27 on How Social Security COLAs are Calculated for more information.)

Unfortunately, the reason behind making this change is the fact that it will ultimately save money for the Social Security system, directly at the expense of the beneficiaries of the system. Here's what you can expect:

As an example, the CPI-W indicates a year-over-year increase from September 2013 to September 2014 of 1.7%. Over the same period, the C-CPI-U only shows an increase of 1.6%.

This is due to the factors used in calculating the C-CPI-U, which considers that as inflation increases spending on certain items will decrease since consumers will purchase cheaper items or less quantity of items as the prices increase. The Bureau of Labor Statistics, which tracks these things and comes up with the indexes, suggests the chained index more accurately reflects the way real-live consumers operate with regard to inflation.

Estimates by the actuaries for the SSA indicate this change could result in a $1,000 per year reduction of benefits (or actually, forgone benefit) by the age of 85. Using the C-CPI-U instead of the CPI-W is estimated to result in a 10% lower total benefit being paid out over a 30-year span.

Each year's increase, if this new index is put into place, is anticipated to be two- to three-tenths of a percent lower than the increase would have been under the current index.

The change in index is not only proposed for Social Security benefits but also for certain tax provisions as well, such as the standard deduction and tax rate tables. In both cases, the taxpayer (at all levels, not just the "rich") will be impacted negatively.

As always, the only way to try to impact this is to contact your representatives in Congress and let them know you're not in favor of having your miniscule increases reduced further in the name of budget cutting. There are plenty of places where pork can be removed from the budget before hitting our seniors with   this,   in   my   opinion.

Index

20/40 Rule *51*
AIME*See* Average Indexed
 Monthly Earnings
Average Indexed Monthly
 Earnings *11*
Average Wage Index *19*
AWI *See* Average Wage Index
bend point 19, *66*
 FMB *39*
calculator-breath 88
COLAs*See* Cost Of Living
 Adjustments
considered retired *62*
Cost Of Living Adjustments *87*
credits*See* Social Security
 credits
deemed filing *29, 125*
Delayed Retirement Credit*24,*
46
Disability Benefits *47*
divorce *7, 112*
Do-Over *103, 105*
DRC*See* Delayed Retirement
 Credit
Earliest Eligibility Age *11*
Earnings Tests *57*
EEA *See* Earliest Eligibility Age
Family Maximum Benefit 39
File and Suspend *121*
FMB*See* Family Maximum
 Benefit
Form W-4V *93*
FRA *See* Full Retirement Age

Full Retirement Age *9*
Government Pension Offset *69*
GPO*See* Government Pension
 Offset
Legislative Bulletin 106-20 *123*
payback *63*
PIA*See* Primary Insurance
 Amount
Primary Insurance Amount *15*
remarriage *111*
Restricted Application 108, *119*
Restricted Application for
 Spousal Benefits*See*
 Restricted Application
Senior Citizens' Freedom to
 Work Act of 2000 *123*
Social Security credit *6*
Spousal Benefit*7, 27, 107, 111,*
117, 121, 129
substantial earnings *67*
substantial services in self-
 employment *62*
surviving parent *37*
Survivor Benefit *31*
WEP*See* Windfall Elimination
 Provision
widow *8, 111, 112*
Windfall Elimination Provision
 65
withdrawal policy *105*
withholding *91*
Zero Year *43*

Acronyms

AIME – Average Indexed Monthly Earnings

AWI – Average Wage Index

COLA – Cost of Living Adjustment

DRC – Delayed Retirement Credits

EEA – Earliest Eligibility Age

F&S – File and Suspend

FMB – Family Maximum Benefit

FRA – Full Retirement Age

GPO – Government Pension Offset

HES – Higher Earning Spouse

LES – Lower Earning Spouse

NH – NumberHolder

PIA – Primary Insurance Amount

SSA – Social Security Administration

SSI – Supplemental Security Income

WEP – Windfall Elimination Provision

Appendix A

Social Security Legislative Bulletin 106-20

See the following web address for a downloadable copy:

www.socialsecurityownersmanual.com/legislative-bulletin-106-20/

106-20

April 7, 2000

The President Signs the "Senior Citizens' Freedom to Work Act of 2000"

Today, President Clinton signed into law P.L. 106-182, the Senior Citizens' Freedom To Work Act of 2000.

As yet, a public law number has not been assigned.

The legislation:

- Eliminates the Social Security retirement earnings test in and after the month in which a person attains full retirement age--currently age 65. Elimination of the retirement test would be effective with respect to taxable years ending after December 31, 1999.
- In the calendar year the beneficiary attains the full retirement age, permanently applies the earnings limit for those at the full retirement age through age 69 ($17,000 in 2000, $25,000 in 2001 and $30,000 in 2002) and the corresponding reduction rate ($1 for $3 offset) to all months prior to attainment of the full retirement age. (In applying the earnings test for this calendar year, only earnings before the month of attainment of full retirement age are considered.)

- Permits, beginning with the month in which the beneficiary reaches full retirement age and ending with the month prior to attainment of age 70, the retired worker to earn a delayed retirement credit for any month for which the retired worker requests that benefits not be paid even though he/she is already on the benefit rolls. On March 1, 2000, the House approved an earlier version of H.R. 5. The Senate approved an amended version of the legislation on March 22, 2000. The House agreed to the Senate amendment to the legislation and cleared the measure for transmission to the President on March 28, 2000. For additional detail, see Legislative Bulletins **106-16, 106-17, 106-18 and 106-19.**